Science Experiments with Arduinos Using a Multi-Function Board

Book 2 in the *Saturday Afternoon Low-Cost Electronics Projects* Series

Eric Bogatin

Addie Rose Press

First Edition

Dec 2019

ISBN 9781734405934

A Publication of Addie Rose Press

Addie Rose Press

Preface: Buy this ebook

If you are looking for the starting place to enter the wonderful world of the Arduino, you should definitely check out the first book in this series, Arduinos without Tears. This is the simplest, easiest and lowest cost entry to get you started with the Arduino.

We introduce you to some of the important tips, tricks and skills you can use if you ever want to advance beyond Blink.

In this second book in the Saturday Afternoon Low-Cost Electronics series, we go the next step.

In keeping with the idea to *minimize the hassle of complicated wiring* and to *provide a very low cost starting place* to do some *pretty cool experiments*, I introduce you to a simple add on board costing less than $3 that has enough sensors and actuators to keep you busy for a dozen open ended science experiments.

All you need for these experiments is an Arduino and this board. I show you where you can get both for less than $5.

You will not find an easier to follow, more in-depth introduction to Arduinos, electronics and science, for as low an investment as this eBook.

Welcome to the wonderful world of Science Experiments with Arduinos.

Check out Eric Bogatin's eBooks in the *Saturday Afternoon Low-Cost Electronics Projects* series:

Book 1: Arduinos without Tears: the ultimate, simplest getting started guide for Arduinos with six experiments in science and coding using nothing more than a low-cost Arduino.

Book 2: Science Experiments with Arduinos Using a Multifunction Board, exploring more than a dozen experiments using the Arduino and a simple add on multi-function board costing about $3. No wiring needed, just plug and play.

Book 3: More Science Experiments with Arduinos Using an LED Accessory Kit: exploring another dozen experiments in science and electronics using the Arduino and a simple kit of parts costing less than $3.

Book 4: Science Experiments with the SparkFun RedBoard Turbo, exploring more than a dozen experiments using the Sparkfun RedBoard Turbo, a high-performance data acquisition Arduino.

Book 5: Three Must Have Instruments for Every Lab: the missing manuals for the Arduino as a voltage source and datalogger, the Digital Multi-Meter (DMM), and the scope/function generator.

Book 6: Electronics You Should Have Learned in High School. Starting with the basics and establishing a firm foundation in current, voltage, resistance and power, simple circuits, voltage sources, I-V curves, diodes, schematics, measuring voltage, current, resistance, voltage dividers, capacitors and inductors.

You can find more details about these and other resources on his author's page on Amazon.com and his author's website, and the HackingPhysics web page.

Better yet, subscribe to the Hacking Physics Journal.

Table of Contents

Chapter 1. A Dozen Science Experiments with Arduinos for less than $4

If you have explored Arduinos a little and are comfortable getting your Arduino to Blink and looking for the next step, you've come to the right place.

In Arduinos Without Tears, we introduce the following coding skills and hardware features through a dozen experiments:

- *Communicating with your Arduino*
- *Writing your own Blink sketch*
- *Writing your own Its Alive sketch*
- *Printing to the serial link*
- *How fast can we send data to the serial monitor?*
- *Modulating the on-board LED*
- *Using and naming variables*
- *Testing persistence of vision*
- *Creating number patterns*
- *Plotting numbers on the serial plotter*
- *If...then commands*
- *For loops*
- *While loops*
- *Random numbers*
- *Calculating random walk patterns*

- *Simulating winning strategies for Roulette*
- *Reading analog voltages*
- *Averaging over a fixed time to reduce 60 Hz pick up*
- *Measuring static fields and static charges*

If you are not familiar with some of these techniques, I strongly recommend you check out Arduinos Without Tears. We will rely on these skills and add to them in this eBook and build your Arduino skills to tackle more challenging projects.

We explore applications of the power of the Arduino to:

- ✓ *measure things*
- ✓ *explore patterns in numbers*
- ✓ *manipulate flashing lights, colors and sounds*
- ✓ *turn the **data** into **information***
- ✓ *use this information to **react and change** the environment.*

We take advantage of a very simple, low-cost board you can purchase for less than $4 which will add inputs and outputs to your basic Arduino. The combination of the Arduino Uno and this board enables us to extend the reach of the simple Arduino board into the physical world of sensors and actuators. With them, we will explore a dozen cool science experiments.

Here are some of the projects on tap in this eBook:

- *Test your reflexes to sound or light stimuli*
- *Calibrate your perception of time flow.*
- *Watch the blood flow through your finger and make an LED pulse to its flow.*

- *Measure temperature and humidity and data log the information into a text file or directly into excel.*
- *Explore the properties of random numbers and see if you can control them with just your mind.*

I will introduce you to and give you practice in skills which will come in handy for these sorts of projects, and many more.

Along the way, I'll introduce you to some of the important elements of doing science experiments. In particular, we'll be *looking under the hood* to understand what is really going on with the sensors, actuators and electronics built into the multi-function board and the Arduino.

This eBook focuses on using Arduinos for science projects that can be completed in a Saturday afternoon.

1.1 Getting started with Arduinos

If you have never used an Arduino, or have never gotten your Arduino to work well, you should check out the first book in this series, Arduinos Without Tears.

I walk you through purchasing an Arduino for less than $4 and getting started with your computer talking to and controlling your Arduino. I introduce some of the basic principles of coding and get you going with a few good habits.

This first book in the series will give you a jump start into the exciting world of Arduinos and arm you with the skills and habits you will use in many future projects.

Using just the Arduino and nothing more, I introduce you to a dozen experiments and projects in which you learn basic coding techniques like printing, plotting, for loops, while loops, variables, pulse width modulation, plotting random numbers and random walks and more.

Here are the commands we introduced in the first book. We leverage many of these commands, features and techniques in this second book in the series.

If you are not familiar with any of these commands, you should check out the first book in this series and explore how to use the command and some examples of sketches where they are introduced.

Command	**Description**

void setup (){
 	
}
	This is a function that appears in EVERY sketch. Every command within the brackets will be executed just once

void loop (){
 	
}
	This is a function that appears in EVERY sketch. Every command within the brackets will execute over and over again.

`pinMode(13, OUTPUT);`	This command tells the Arduino that we are going to use a specific digital pin as an `OUTPUT`, as distinct from an `INPUT`. We use the pin number to identify the pin we want to setup.
`digitalWrite(13, HIGH);`	This command controls the output of a digital pin and makes it either a `HIGH` (logic 1, or 5 V) or a `LOW` (a logic 0 or a 0 V). Once executed, the pin value will be set to this value.

`delay(1000);`	This command tells the Arduino to sit there, twiddling its thumbs, doing nothing for a duration of milliseconds as listed inside the (). In this example, the time interval to wait is 1000 msec = 1 sec.
// or /* */	Comments. Everything after these two forward slashes will be ignored by the Arduino sketch. We can use this add comments for our own benefit on any line. For multiple lines add them between the /* and the */ lines.
`Serial.begin(9600);`	This command opens up the serial com link with a baud rated inside the (). In this example the baud rate is 9600 baud. The name `Serial` is an object, the serial link. The `.begin` is a verb, telling the object to get set up.
`Serial.print("Hello World");`	This command will print characters to the serial communications channel. Everything inside the () will be printed. To print a string, enclose the characters within quotes. After printing, the cursor will be left on the same line.
`Serial.println(" ");`	Does the same thing as the `Serial.print` command, but moves the cursor to the next line after printing the characters. This starts the next printed content on a new line.

Serial monitor	The terminal emulator that you can print to. This is the primary way of displaying information from the Arduino.
`int, long`	This will create a new variable that will store an integer. This is a whole number. It is usually placed before the setup() function
`float`	This will create a new variable that will store a floating-point number. This is a number that has a decimal point. It is usually placed before the setup() function
`+, -, *, / =`	Simple algebra
`==`	A conditional test: are the two terms on either side of the == the same. Not a misprint, double equal signs.
`if (iVal == 1) { }`	If conditional. If the statement inside the () is true, then the commands between the brackets are executed.
Tools/Autoformat	Will add indents and clean up the look of your code
Serial Plotter	A built-in graphing features which plots the numbers printed to serial com port.
`for (index = 1; index <= npts; index = index + 1) { //execute this code }`	For loop. There are three statements inside the () of the for loop. The first sets the initial value of the index. The second term is the condition. If the condition is true, continue in the loop, otherwise, leave the loop. The third term is the increment. The code inside the {} is executed in the loop.

`random(min, max)`	Returns a random, long integer number between min and (max-1).
randomSeed()	This term will start the random number generator with the number inside the ().
analogRead(pinNumber);	The command to read the voltage, in units of ADU, from 0 to 1023, from the analog pin, pinNumber.

`while (x < 10) {`
`  //Execute this code`
`}`
	While loop. Another type of loop which will repeat everything inside the {} as long as the statement inside the () is true.

1.2 My workshops

I've been teaching Arduino workshops to folks from 8 years old to 80 years old, some of whom never touched an Arduino before, and some who tried to get started but stopped in frustration. In Figure 1.1 is a picture of one of my workshops at TinkerMill, our hackerspace in Longmont, CO.

Figure 1.1. Example of one of my Arduino workshops at Tinkermill, a hackerspace in Longmont, CO.

I have found in my workshops that one of the biggest sources of frustration, especially for folks just starting out, is having to deal with a lot of jumper wires from the Arduino to other boards and sensors. As you can see in Figure 1.2 this can get very complicated, very quickly.

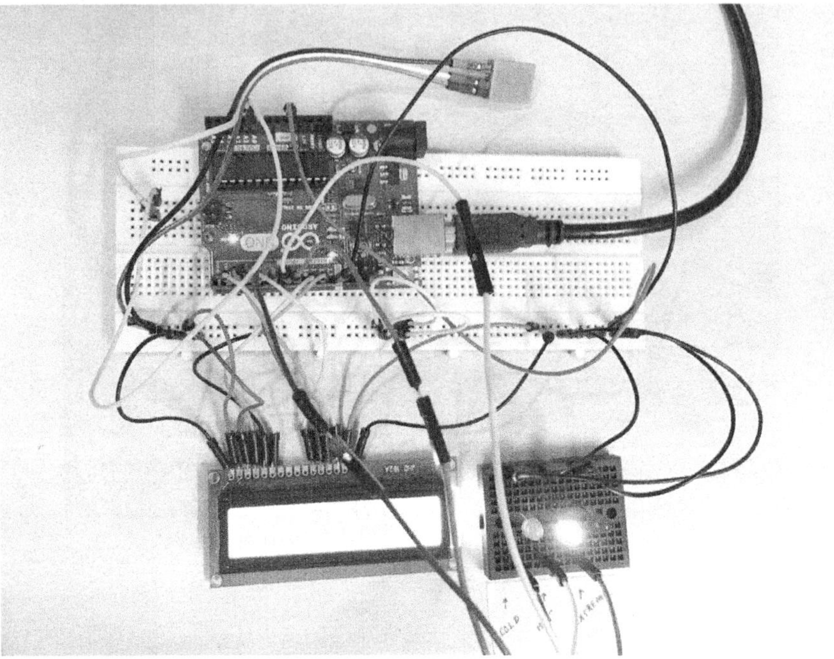

Figure 1.2 Example of an Arduino project with lots of confusing jumper wires.

This eBook, and all the examples we do, ***require no jumper wires***. All the projects use a simple add-on board, called a shield, which already has a number of sensors and actuators connected to it.

When plugged into the Arduino board, these sensors connect automatically to the analog and digital I/O pins. Using this *plug and play* multi-function board, we dramatically lower the frustration level in all the experiments illustrated here. The goal is to get to the cool part of the experiments, as soon as possible.

1.3 Understand by doing

Many will say that "*you learn by doing.*" I don't think this is quite correct.

I think you learn by studying, by reviewing the essential principles, and by reviewing lectures, textbooks, and lots of examples.

I think you ***understand*** by doing. The purpose of solving problems is to exercise your understanding. You see the principles in action when you work problems.

The motto of the Interactive Technology Learning Lab (ITLL) at the University of Colorado, Boulder, is shown in

Figure 1.3 The motto of the ITLL at University of Colorado, Boulder. "I hear, I forget. I see, I remember. I do and I understand," a quote by Confucius, 500 BC

But, just ***doing***, isn't enough.

If you simulate or build something by just following some canned directions and just "*try it and see*", I think you learn little and understand less. It is just play, which is okay, it's just not *accelerating you up the learning curve.*

These activities: building, measuring and simulating, require active participation to get you the most value and exercise your understanding.

I push my students to apply Rule #9 to everything they do. This is the most important principle in engineering and is a good habit for everyone.

> ***Rule #9 is: Never do a measurement or simulation without first anticipating what you expect to see. If you are wrong, there is a reason for it. Do not proceed until you investigate the reason and either fix the problem or understand why you were wrong. If you were right, you get a nice warm feeling that maybe you do understand what is going on. It is an important confidence builder.***

The guiding principle here is to exercise your understanding at every chance. Think about what should happen before you do it and see if it works the way you expect.

When you build a circuit or write a sketch, think about what you expect to see. Use the principles you have learned to anticipate how the world you have created should behave. Then test it out.

Does what you expect, happen? If it does, feel good about your accomplishment. You understand how to apply the essential principles. If it doesn't respond the way you expected, investigate why. Is the project set up the way you think it is? Are the connections correct? Is this a chance to refine your understanding?

We will try to take every opportunity to exercise Rule #9 throughout this eBook. Using the Arduino with its accessories will provide many examples of building projects which interface between the physical world, with electronics, with coding and with microcontrollers. This is the world of *physical computing*.

1.4 No assembly required!

The chief driving force for this eBook is to get you started using Arduinos to do some real science as quickly as possible without getting bogged down in a lot of complicated wiring.

The complicated wiring can come later when you have more experience and need to do the wiring. And then, I'll give you some pointers how to do it right with good habits that will give you a better chance of getting your project working the first time.

I reviewed many add-on products for the Arduino and settled on this multi-function board because it is really easy to use, has some cool components and is so low cost.

Every experiment in this eBook can be done with either the Arduino board by itself or with just this add on shield that plugs directly into the Arduino. It is the perfect starter kit for your Arduino projects. Figure 1.4 shows the multi-function board plugged into the Arduino board. This is the way we will use this add-on shield.

Figure 1.4. The multi-function board literally just plugs into the Arduino board. That's all the assembly required.

1.5 The low-cost multi-function board for all these projects

I've scoured the Internet to find simple, low-cost kits which add a lot of functionality to the Arduino and are really easy to use.

The Arduino itself is really just a platform to measure voltages coming in and create some voltage signals that go out. There's a lot we can do with just these features, like measure static electricity or test for randomness in random numbers.

An Arduino board itself really only has its on-board LED to create an output other than a voltage. We explored some simple projects we can do with this on-board LED in the first eBook in this series, Arduino without Tears.

We used the Arduino as a computer to off-load computations to the little microcontroller and send back the final results which were displayed or plotted. With the Arduino as a computer, we explored random numbers and simulated random walk trajectories, plotted on the built-in serial plotter.

The one thing we were able to measure with just the Arduino, using no other additional parts, was static electric fields. These fields are all around us, but especially when we get charged up by walking on a carpet, petting a cat, moving in our chair or even opening up a Velcro strap.

If you want more details about these experiments, check out Arduinos without Tears.

Add to the Arduino board some external sensors and actuators and we can record voltages from sensors and use the output voltages to control lights, sounds and actions.

As a microcontroller and a "*gateway drug*" to the world of physical computing, we will concentrate in this eBook on connecting the Arduino board to other elements to measure sensors and doing stuff with that information.

The multi-function board I found for this series of experiments:

- ✓ *is very low-cost*
- ✓ *requires no wiring of any sort*
- ✓ *contains enough variety to provide hours of exciting science projects*
- ✓ *is re-usable for many future projects*

Best of all, it costs less than $4, shipping included, and enables a large assortment of frustration-free projects.

1.6 Purchase ALL the parts you will need for this Book

All of the experiments in this book can be completed with just the simple Arduino board and USB cable and the multi-function add on board. You will need NOTHING else. Here is a quick link to purchase these items if you do not already have one:

<table>
<tr>
<td></td>
<td>Arduino Uno with USB cable.

Price is about $3.00 to $3.75, shipping included.

Purchase from this link, for example.

If it is no longer available, you can do a search on www.aliexpress for Arduino Uno R3 and select any vendor.</td>
</tr>
</table>

	The multi-function shield. Price is about $3.15 to $3.75, shipping included. You can purchase it from here. If it is not available, search www.aliexpress.com for Multifunction Expansion Board DHT11 or click here and select any unit that looks like this one.

The multifunction board, shown in Figure 1.5, can be purchased for less than $4, shipping included.

Figure 1.5 The multi-function board we will use for all the projects in this eBook.

The one downside of purchasing this kit from this web site and at this incredibly low price is that the delivery time can be as long as 30-60 days.

Place your order early.

This is a popular Arduino Shield. There are other web sites from which you can purchase this board. But the price will vary from $4 to $21, for exactly the same board. If you want your board soon, spending more may be worth it. Part of the value you are purchasing at the higher price is time.

Chapter 2. The multifunction board overview

There are a number of multi-function boards designed to plug directly into the Arduino and provide additional, specialized functions.

The chief advantage of these plug-in boards, usually referred to as *shields*, is that ***no wiring is required***. All the connections are made automatically by the pins that plug into the Arduino. Figure 2.1 shows an example of the multi-function board plugged into an Arduino.

Figure 2.1 The multi-function board plugged into the Arduino board. That's the only assembly required.

I chose this specific multi-function board because it has a good selection of sensors and actuators and because it is very low cost. No other product with this number of features comes close to this low a price.

Here is what comes on the board:

Input devices: sensors

- *two momentary closed switches*
- *a temperature/humidity smart sensor*
- *IR sensor (like on a remote control)*
- *two digital input ports*
- *a resistor potentiometer*
- *a photo-resistor*
- *a LM35 temperature sensor (may not work on your board)*
- *an analog input port*

Output devices: actuators

- *a fixed frequency buzzer*
- *a 3-color LED*
- *a red LED*
- *a blue LED*

All this multi-function board does is connect the various sensors and actuators to specific analog or digital pins. They are all passive connections. It is just like if we had connected all the components into a solderless breadboard and used jumper cables from the Arduino pins to the components.

But then we would have a huge array of wires looping from the Arduino board to the solderless breadboard. It can get complicated quickly and hard to debug unless you are skilled in electronics and wiring.

The multi-function board provides a substrate to mount the components and connects them to the appropriate Arduino pins. There is no microcontroller on the multi-function board, and no smart interface; there are only components individually connected to the Arduino.

In this way, the multi-function board is literally just a bunch of individual components that could have plugged into a solderless breadboard.

The first step is to be aware of what is connected to which pins. Before we use any device in an experiment, we will test it by writing a simple sketch and verify its performance.

Here are the pin connections to the multi-function board:

Table 2-1 The pin assignment for the multi-function board and the Arduino pins.

Pin number	***device***
Digital pin 2	Switch D2
Digital pin 3	Switch D3
Digital pin 4	DHT11 temperature/humidity sensor
Digital pin 5	buzzer
Digital pin 6	IR remote sensor
Digital pin 7	Digital I/O port
Digital pin 8	Digital I/O port
Digital pin 9	3-color LED-red
Digital pin 10	3-color LED-green
Digital pin 11	3-color LED-blue
Digital pin 12	LED red
Digital pin 13	LED blue

Analog pin A0	resistor pot
Analog pin A1	photo sensor
Analog pin A2	LM35 temperature sensor
Analog pin A3	analog port in

2.1 Sketch: "*Hello World*" for your multi-function board

It is traditional, in a new board, to show in some way that it is working or "*alive*". When turning on a computer or microcontroller for the first time, we usually have it print out the message, "*Hello World.*"

In the first book of this series, Arduinos Without Tears, we show an alternative to printing "Hello World" by having the Arduino display a heartbeat.

For our multifunction board, since it is not a microcontroller, we'll use the same indicator to show that the multi-function board is *alive,* and have it display a heartbeat.

The idea is to blink the red LED like the pulsing of a heartbeat.

Arduino digital pins 13 and 12 are connected to LEDs on the multi-function board in series with on-board 200 Ohm resistors. These two LEDs are circled in Figure 2.2.

Figure 2.2 The multi-function board showing the red and blue LEDs.

Digital pin 13 is connected to the blue LED and digital pin 12 is connected to the red LED.

We'll make our multi-function board come alive by showing a heartbeat pattern on the red LED. Red seems appropriate. This is the microcontroller equivalent of "Hello World."

If you have a little experience with Arduinos, you should be able to write a sketch to blink the pin 13 LED on the Arduino board. If you don't know where to start, check out Arduinos Without Tears.

We will make two modifications to the simple Blink sketch. First, we will be addressing pin 12, not pin 13. It's digital pin 12 that has the red LED on the multi-function board. I just think a red LED makes a better heartbeat than a blue LED.

The second modification from Blink is to add another *thump* step. We want the blinking pattern to be thump-thump, ..., thump-

thump....thump-thump, like a heartbeat. I think this is a little cooler than just blink...blink...blink.

Try this experiment: Think about how you would write the sketch for this heartbeat on pin 12.

If you get stuck, take a look at the sketch I wrote below. While you can literally copy the code below from this pdf and paste it into a blank sketch, upload it and it will run, I recommend you type in the code, line by line. This will help you build the muscle memory and make you a better coder.

I think the process of typing in the code for each example sketch is a really good habit. It helps build muscle memory and will help you be a better coder in the long term.

But, if you want to see the LED flash NOW!, go right ahead and copy and paste.

While our goal is to get the red LED on the multi-function board to beat like a heartbeat, as a Best Design Practice to aid in debugging systems, it's always useful to start with something either simple or you have high confidence is going to work, and then add complexity.

Before we plug in the multi-function board, let's get the heartbeat working on the Arduino board alone to verify the code is working and the computer can talk to the Arduino.

Here is the sketch we created in the first book in this series, Arduinos Without Tears to make the on-board LED thump like a heartbeat:

```
//it's alive
void setup() {
```

```
  pinMode(13, OUTPUT);
}

void loop() {
  digitalWrite(13, HIGH);
  delay(100);
  digitalWrite(13, LOW);
  delay(100);
  digitalWrite(13, HIGH);
  delay(100);
  digitalWrite(13, LOW);
  delay(500);
}
```

There are only a few simple code elements in this sketch, which you should know. A summary listing of the basic code elements you should be familiar with which are used in this sketch is at the end of this chapter.

We will add to this table in each chapter as we add new code elements. Of course, all of them can be found in the reference page of the Arduino IDE.

To understand this simple sketch, we take advantage of the following code elements, introduced in the first book in the series:

`pinMode(13, OUTPUT);` tells the Arduino to set up digital pin 13 as a digital output

`digitalWrite(13, HIGH);` tells the Arduino to make the output of digital pin 13 a HIGH which is the same as turn the voltage on to the full 5 V.

`delay(100);` wait at this line, doing nothing except twiddling your thumbs for 100 msec, which is 0.1 sec, then move to the next line.

To run this sketch on your Arduino and test out the multi-function board, here are the steps.

Step 1 is to make sure this will run on your Arduino and thump the on-board LED. At this point, DO NOT plug your multi-function board into your Arduino.

1. *Open the Arduino IDE and a sketch will open up.*
2. *Under File, select new and a blank sketch will open up.*
3. *Highlight the content of the sketch and then delete all the content so it is completely empty.*
4. *Copy the sketch above out of the ebook or pdf version of this eBook.*
5. *Paste it into the blank sketch.*
6. *It is ready to run!*
7. *Verify you have the correct board and port number selected.*
8. *Click the upload button (right pointing arrow).*

If this sketch works the first time, great, you have verified your computer is talking to your Arduino, the Arduino is working and pin 13 is modulating off and on.

If it doesn't work as expected, there is something not working, related to the Arduino board, and, since it is not connected yet, ***not related*** to the multi-function board.

This is an example of an important *Best Design Practice* in any debug process:

Test pieces of your project as you go, to confirm it is working before assembling everything. Don't wait to turn on your entire, complex system and find it doesn't work. It will be much more difficult to debug.

Build and test in parts or subsections as you go, gaining confidence in each part.

Upload this sketch to your Arduino. If the on-board LED works, step 1 is done.

Step 2 is to plug the multi-function board into the Arduino. The blue LED connected to digital pin 13 should throb like a heartbeat. If it does, it means at least the connection from pin 13 to the blue LED is working.

Step 3 is to change the pin 13 in the sketch to pin 12 and watch the red LED on the multi-function board throb like a heartbeat. If you see this, then you have successfully tested the connection between your computer and the Arduino and at least two connections to the multifunction board.

If this last step works, congratulations! You can communicate from your computer to the Arduino and multi-function board.

We'll try other tests as we introduce each sensor and actuator.

2.2 Organization of This eBook

In the following chapters, we introduce new Arduino features, new sensor and actuator features, new electronics principles and new coding features by way of experiments.

Oh, and we use the power of physical computing to conduct some really cool science experiments, each of which could fill an afternoon with activity.

In each chapter, we identify the new principles or techniques by the prefaces: New Code, New Techniques, New Hardware. This way, if there is a specific topic you want to explore, you can browse the table of contents and find where we introduce this concept.

We leverage many of these new techniques in follow-on chapters.

2.3 Summary of all the commands introduced so far

Command	Description

`void setup(){`
 	
`}`
	This is a function that appears in EVERY sketch. Every command within the brackets will be executed just once

`void loop(){`
 	
`}`
	This is a function that appears in EVERY sketch. Every command within the brackets will execute over and over again.

`pinMode(13, OUTPUT);`	This command tells the Arduino that we are going to use a specific digital pin as an `OUTPUT`, as distinct from an `INPUT`. We use the pin number to identify the pin we want to setup.
`digitalWrite(13, HIGH);`	This command controls the output of a digital pin and makes it either a `HIGH` (logic 1, or 5 V) or a `LOW` (a logic 0 or a 0 V). Once executed, the pin value will be set to this value.
`delay(1000);`	This command tells the Arduino to sit there, twiddling its thumbs, doing nothing for a duration of milliseconds as listed inside the (). In this example, the time interval to wait is 1000 msec = 1 sec.

// or /* */	Comments. Everything after these two forward slashes will be ignored by the Arduino sketch. We can use this add comments for our own benefit on any line. For multiple lines add them between the /* and the */ lines.
`Serial.begin(9600);`	This command opens up the serial com link with a baud rated inside the (). In this example the baud rate is 9600 baud. The name `Serial` is an object, the serial link. The `.begin` is a verb, telling the object to get set up.
`Serial.print("Hello World");`	This command will print characters to the serial communications channel. Everything inside the () will be printed. To print a string, enclose the characters within quotes. After printing, the cursor will be left on the same line.
`Serial.println(" ");`	Does the same thing as the `Serial.print` command, but moves the cursor to the next line after printing the characters. This starts the next printed content on a new line.
Serial monitor	The terminal emulator that you can print to. This is the primary way of displaying information from the Arduino.
`int, long`	This will create a new variable that will store an integer. This is a whole number. It is usually placed before the setup() function

float	This will create a new variable that will store a floating-point number. This is a number that has a decimal point. It is usually placed before the setup() function
+, -, *, / =	Simple algebra
==	A conditional test: are the two terms on either side of the == the same. Not a misprint, double equal signs.
if (iVal == 1) { }	If conditional. If the statement inside the () is true, then the commands between the brackets are executed.
Tools/Autoformat	Will add indents and clean up the look of your code
Serial Plotter	A built-in graphing features which plots the numbers printed to serial com port.

for (index = 1; index <= npts; index = index + 1) {
  //execute this code
}
	For loop. There are three statements inside the () of the for loop. The first sets the initial value of the index. The second term is the condition. If the condition is true, continue in the loop, otherwise, leave the loop. The third term is the increment. The code inside the {} is executed in the loop.

random(min, max)	Returns a random, long integer number between min and (max-1).
randomSeed()	This term will start the random number generator with the number inside the ().

analogRead(pinNumber);	The command to read the voltage, in units of ADU, from 0 to 1023, from the analog pin, pinNumber.

`while (x < 10) {`
`  //Execute this code`
`}`
	While loop. Another type of loop which will repeat everything inside the {} as long as the statement inside the () is true.

Chapter 3. Make A Million Different Colors

In this experiment, we're going to adjust the *apparent* brightness of an LED not by changing its DC current directly, but by changing the duty cycle of a pulse train that drives it.

If we modulate the LED faster than our flicker rate, the LED will look continuously on. We can then adjust the duty cycle to change its brightness. This is called pulse width modulation (PWM).

When we change the apparent brightness of three different color LEDs, we can make any color at all.

3.1 Pulse train and Blink

In Arduinos without Tears, we introduced the idea of a pulse train defined by a period and duty cycle. As long as the period was short enough, the LED looked like it was on all the time and not flashing. The duty cycle controlled the apparent brightness.

We wrote a simple sketch where we entered the period and duty cycle using variables and translated this in terms of delay times. The actual voltage to the LED and the pattern of on-and-off times is illustrated in Figure 3.1.

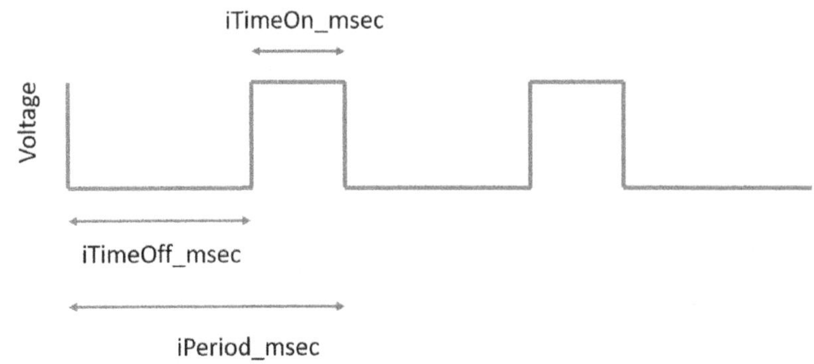

$$DutyCycle = \frac{iTimeOn\_msec}{iPeriod\_msec}$$

Figure 3.1. The pattern of on and off times of the LED when it is modulated.

We can modulate any LED with this pattern. This is, after all, what we did in the BLINK sketch. To control the LED on and off times, we used a delay time to keep the LED in the HIGH state and a different delay time to keep the LED in the LOW state.

While these are the terms we used in the Blink sketch, it was an awkward way of describing a pulse train. It would be much more convenient if we described the pulse train in terms of the period and the duty cycle.

This way, we select a period short enough to be below the flicker rate, and then just adjust the duty cycle to change the brightness.

3.2 A pulse train and its duty cycle

I like using the period and duty cycle to control the LED. This is a more intuitive set of figures of merit. To modulate the LED, and use the principles of the BLINK code, we will need to translate the period and duty cycle into the on and off times.

This is very simple. The on-time and off-time are:

onTime_sec = Period_sec x dutyCycle

offTime_sec = Period_sec x (1-dutyCycle)

The duty cycle controls the apparent brightness of the LED. A duty cycle of 90% means the LED is on for most of the period and it will look bright to us. A duty cycle of only 10% means the LED is on for only a small fraction of the period and it will look dim to our eye.

We will modulate the LED with a period that is short enough so that our eye can't tell the LED is pulsing off and on.

To make the LED flash fast enough so we can't see it flashing, we want the period to be shorter than about 38 msec, or the flash frequency to be faster than 1/38 msec = 26 Hz.

This means we can adjust the on-time from 0 msec to 38 msec. We use delay() commands to adjust the on and off times.

A modified BLINK is all we need to drive the LED with a pulse train. We'll start with a period of 0.038 seconds (38 msec) and adjust the duty cycle from 0% to 100%.

Try this experiment: How would you write the code to set the period and duty cycle for the LED?

3.3 Sketch: Modulating an LED with period and duty cycle control

Here is my code to modulate the LED on pin 13 using the period and duty cycle figures of merit:

```
float Period_sec = 0.038;
float dutyCycle = 0.1;
int pinLED = 13;
```

```
float onTime_sec = Period_sec * dutyCycle;
float offTime_sec = Period_sec * (1.0 - dutyCycle);
/////////////////////////////////////
void setup() {
  pinMode(pinLED, OUTPUT);
}

void loop() {
  digitalWrite(pinLED, HIGH);
  delay(onTime_sec * 1000);
  digitalWrite(pinLED, LOW);
  delay(offTime_sec * 1000);
}
```

Try this experiment: We can watch the LED turn off and on if we make the period very slow, like 2 second. Then we can see the short or long flashes of the LED during each 2 second period as we adjust the duty cycle.

After you have watched the LED turn off and on slowly, make the period 0.05 second and it will look like the LED is always on, but its brightness changes.

What is the longest period you would be comfortable with to see the light flicker free?

In this example, we created the drive signal manually. It takes a lot of coding overhead the way we did it, and we can only modulate one LED at a time using this method. Luckily, once we understand what is going on, we can use an automated method to do the same thing.

So far, we used pin 13, which is the blue LED. Change the pin to 12 and flash the red LED.

3.4 New Code: analogWrite() and pulse width modulation (PWM)

There are a few special pins on the Arduino which are designed for pulse width modulation. In the Arduino Uno, these pins are digital pins 3, 5, 6, 9, 10 and 11.

Pins 3, 9, 10 and 11 will modulate the output pin at 490 Hz. Pins 5 and 6 will modulate the pin at 980 Hz.

These pins are special. They are called pulse width modulation (PWM) pins. On the Arduino board, they are usually labeled with a small squiggly line in front of the pin number, as seen in Figure 3.2.

Figure 3.2. The Arduino Uno showing the digital pins in the upper row, with the small squiggly lines in front of 3, 5, 6, 9, 10 and 11. These are the PWM digital pins.

The frequency at which these pins switch is fixed. What we get to control is the duty cycle, the fraction of time they are on, or high.

The way we control the duty cycle is with the `analogWrite()` command.

There really is no true analog output on the Arduino. Instead, there is the PWM output. When we control the duty cycle, we are adjusting the average output voltage.

In the analogWrite () command, we specify the duty cycle using an 8-bit number. This means the value can span from 0 to 255 different levels. These levels correspond to an average voltage range of 0 V to 5 V.

The syntax for the command is:

```
analogWrite(11,127);
```

The "pin" is the digital pin number, 3, 5, 6, 9, 10 or 11. The "value" is an integer from 0 to 255. This value corresponds to the duty cycle, with 0 being always off and 255 being always on.

To drive a signal on digital pin 10 that produces a duty cycle of 30% would mean writing a value of 255 x 0.3 = 76. The command would be:

```
analogWrite (10,76);
```

The actual signal coming off of pin 10 would be modulated at 490 Hz, and on for 30% of the time. I connected my Analog Discovery scope to this pin and measured the voltage waveform shown in Figure 3.3.

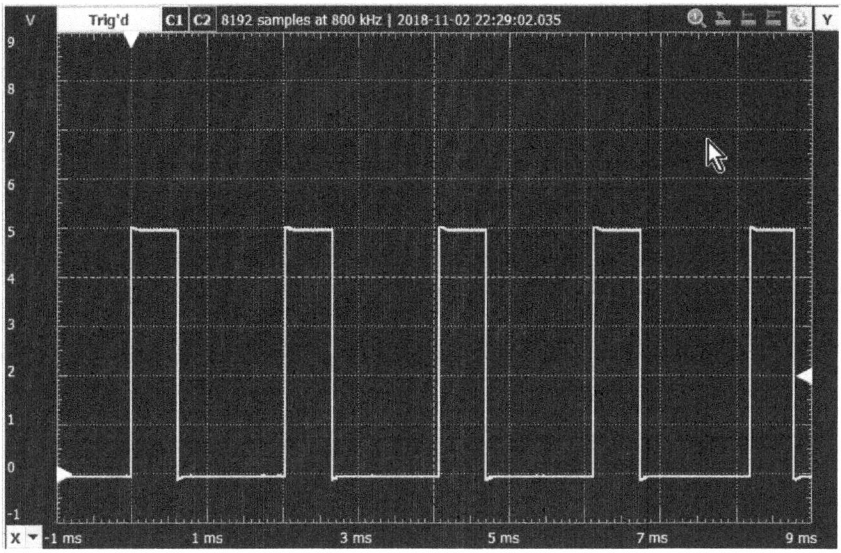

Figure 3.3. The measured voltage on pin 10 when driving a PWM signal set to a value of 76 out of 255.

A significant advantage of using one of the PWM pins is that the pulse train is continually generated once we send the analogWrite () command. After this single command, we can let the code do some other operations and we will always see this digital pulse train on the digital pin.

If we used the manual modulation method, we would have to devote all of our coding to just drive the digital pulses on one pin.

The limitation of the analogWrite method is that there are only the six specific pins that can drive the PWM signal. And, we only have a resolution of up to 255 different levels.

Usually, these are minor inconveniences compared to not requiring any coding overhead to generate six independent PWM signals.

We are armed with a technique to change the brightness of an LED connected to one of the special digital pins. We can apply this new method to change the brightness of each of the three colors, part of a special 3-color LED.

3.5 The 3-color LED and pulse width modulation (PWM)

On the multi-function board, the small white square with a clear plastic cap is the three-color LED. This is circled in Figure 3.4. The three different LEDs are mounted very close to each other in the same package. They are so close together, they look like they are on top of each other.

Figure 3.4. The three-color LED has a red, green and blue integrated into a single LED housing. They are connected to digital pins D9 (red), D10 (blue) and D11 (green).

We drive each of the three colors independently by turning on the digital pins to which each are connected. First, let's make sure we can drive each LED separately.

Here is the connection between each digital pin and the LED color in the 3-color LED:

- *red: pin 9*
- *blue: pin 10*
- *green: pin 11*

Try this experiment: Write the code to blink each of the three colors separately to test out the connections. Turn each color on for 1 second, then off and cycle around the three colors and let this pattern repeat.

Here is my sketch to do this:

```
void setup() {
  pinMode(9, OUTPUT);   //red
  pinMode(10, OUTPUT); //blue
  pinMode(11, OUTPUT);   //green
}
void loop() {
  digitalWrite(9, HIGH);
  delay(1000);
  digitalWrite(9, LOW);
  digitalWrite(10, HIGH);
  delay(1000);
  digitalWrite(10, LOW);
  digitalWrite(11, HIGH);
  delay(1000);
  digitalWrite(11, LOW);
}
```

Try this experiment: Turn on pairs of LEDs at the same time and make note of the new color you see. Then, try turning all three colors on at the same time. What color do you see?

- *What color is equal amounts of red and green?*
- *What color is green and blue?*
- *What color is red and blue?*

If each LED is driven separately, we see the primary colors. If we drive a few of them simultaneously, we can synthesize other colors. By modulating each pin with a PWM signal we can make almost any color by combinations of these three colors, each at a different intensity level.

3.6 Making more than sixteen million colors

If each LED can be modulated at 256 different levels and we have three different, independent LEDs, we could make a total of

256 x 256 x 256 = 16,777,000 colors

Any of these more than 16 million colors can be described with three 8-bit numbers, one for each of the red, green and blue colors.

Since each color can be modulated at 8-bit resolution and there are combinations of three different 8-bit combinations, we sometimes refer to the different colors as 24-bit color.

This is a standard way of defining any color, referred to as RGB colors. Every color is defined by the bit level for the red, green and blue colors.

There are many web sites with examples of the RGB values for every color imaginable. For example, this site lists a variety of RGB values for many colors.

The table in Figure 3.5 offers a few colors and their RGB values. We can use this table to cycle through a few colors.

RGB color table

Basic colors:

Color	HTML / CSS Name	Hex Code #RRGGBB	Decimal Code (R,G,B)
	Black	#000000	(0,0,0)
	White	#FFFFFF	(255,255,255)
	Red	#FF0000	(255,0,0)
	Lime	#00FF00	(0,255,0)
	Blue	#0000FF	(0,0,255)
	Yellow	#FFFF00	(255,255,0)
	Cyan / Aqua	#00FFFF	(0,255,255)
	Magenta / Fuchsia	#FF00FF	(255,0,255)
	Silver	#C0C0C0	(192,192,192)
	Gray	#808080	(128,128,128)
	Maroon	#800000	(128,0,0)
	Olive	#808000	(128,128,0)
	Green	#008000	(0,128,0)
	Purple	#800080	(128,0,128)
	Teal	#008080	(0,128,128)
	Navy	#000080	(0,0,128)

Figure 3.5. Examples of a few colors and their RGB values.

Try this experiment: How would you set up a sketch to define a specific color by its RGB values and then drive the 3-color LED to display the color?

3.7 Sketch: Make 16 million colors

Here is my sketch:

```
int pinR = 9;
int pinG = 11;
int pinB = 10;

///////define the color here:////
int Red = 255;
```

```
int Green = 255;
int Blue = 0;

void setup() {
  pinMode(pinR, OUTPUT);   //red
  pinMode(pinG, OUTPUT); //blue
  pinMode(pinB, OUTPUT);   //green
}

void loop() {
  analogWrite(pinR, Red);
  analogWrite(pinG, Green);
  analogWrite(pinB, Blue);
}
```

Try this experiment: Now that we can make any color, write a sketch that will generate any one of the 16 million colors randomly and keep it on for about 500 msec.

```
int pinR = 9;
int pinG = 11;
int pinB = 10;

void setup() {
  pinMode(pinR, OUTPUT);   //red
  pinMode(pinG, OUTPUT); //blue
  pinMode(pinB, OUTPUT);   //green
}

void loop() {
  ///////define the color here:////
  int Red = random(0, 256);
  int Green = random(0, 256);
  int Blue = random(0, 256);

  analogWrite(pinR, Red);
  analogWrite(pinG, Green);
  analogWrite(pinB, Blue);
  delay(500);
}
```

This sketch will cycle through every color possible, pausing ½ second between colors.

3.8 New Hardware: The resistor pot and analog input

Built onto the multi-function board is a blue resistor pot. The resistor pot is shown in Figure 3.6.

Figure 3.6. The multi-function board with the resistor pot circled.

The two outer leads of the resistor pot are connected to the 5 V power rail and to ground. The center slider is connected to analog pin A0. This circuit is illustrated in Figure 3.7.

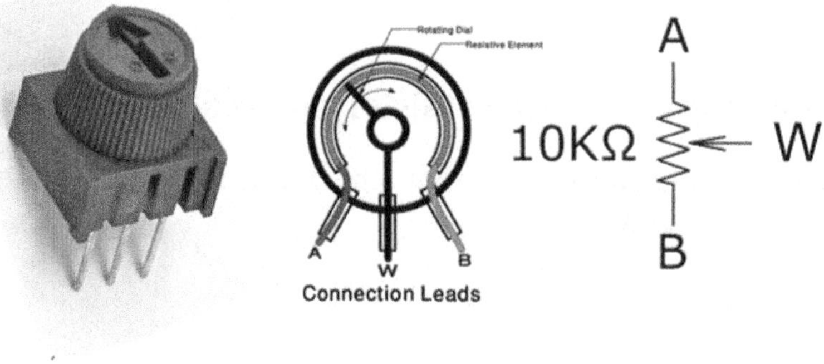

Figure 3.7. An illustration of the resistor pot, its insides and the circuit diagram. Pin A is connected to 5 V, pin B to gnd and pin W, the wiper pin, to the analog pin A0.

When the wiper is mostly rotated counterclockwise (CCW), the wiper pin, W, is next to pin A and the voltage on pin W, will read nearly 5 V compared to gnd. As the knob rotates clockwise (CW), the voltage on the wiper pin, W, will reduce and get closer to 0 V

On the multi-function board, the wiper pin, W, is connected to the analog pin, A0. The voltage we read on analog pin A0 will be a voltage we control with the knob. All we have to do is read the voltage on pin A0 using the

```
analogRead(A0);
```

command.

The analog to digital converter (ADC) on the ATMEGA 328 microcontroller on the Arduino board will measure the voltage on the analog pins. It converts the voltage in a range from 0 V to 5 V into an integer with 1024 different levels. This is a 10-bit resolution, $1024 = 2^{10}$.

When we call the analogRead command, it returns an integer from 0 to 1023. In one line we can literally read the analog voltage and print it to the serial monitor, or plot it on the serial plotter.

Here is the entire sketch to read the analog pin and print it. I added a short delay to slow the acquisition down to see it come out on the screen:

```
void setup() {
  Serial.begin(2000000);
}
void loop() {
  Serial.println(analogRead(A0));
  delay(10);
}
```

When this sketch runs, we can display the numbers on the serial monitor, or plot them on the serial plotter. Figure 3.8 shows the measured voltage on the analog A0 pin, as I rotated knob.

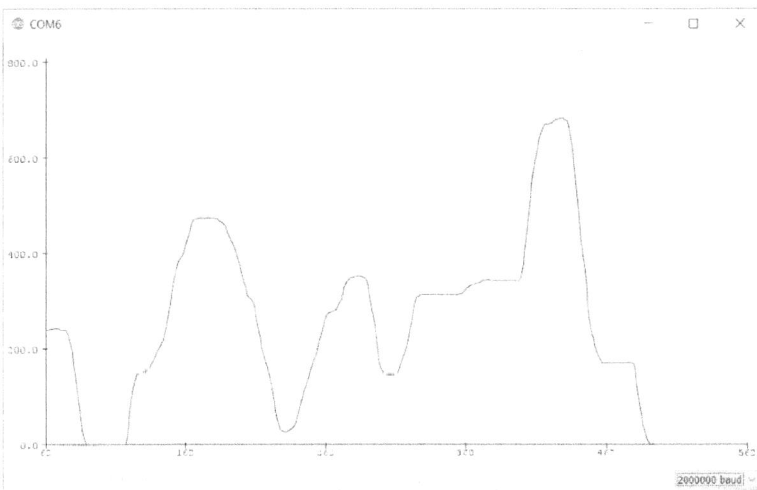

Figure 3.8. Example of the ADU value from the ADC as I turned the resistor pot.

3.9 Feedback: controlling the color with a resistor pot

We can use the input from the analog knob to control an output. In this experiment, we will use the voltage measured on the resistor pot to control the color of the 3-color LED.

A common way of using colors to indicate linear values is through a *color temperature.* On this scale blue, being a low temperature, corresponds to a low voltage, while a redder color corresponds to a higher temperature or a higher voltage.

We need an algorithm to translate the voltage value measured on the ADC pin from 0 to 1023, into an 8-bit color range. The simplest mapping of a 10-bit number into an 8-bit number is to just the divide the 10-bit number by 4.

As the blue light intensity decreases, we want the red-light intensity to increase. While the blue color goes from B = 255 down to B = 0, we want the red intensity to go from R = 0 to R = 255.

The plan would be to have a measured 0 V write the color blue. B = 255, R = 0. Then, by the time we reach 5 V, the colors have flipped and B = 0 and R =255.

How would you write this algorithm?

Try this experiment: You are armed with all the information you need to write a simple sketch that measures the voltage on the pot, divides this value by 4 and writes it to the red and blue LEDs to use the pot to control the color temperature.

3.10 Sketch: controlling a color with a resistor pot

Here is my version of this sketch:

```
int pinPot = A0;
int Pot_ADU;
int pinRed = 9;
int pinGreen = 11;
int pinBlue = 10;

void setup() {
  pinMode(pinRed, OUTPUT);   //red
  pinMode(pinGreen, OUTPUT); //blue
```

```
  pinMode(pinBlue, OUTPUT);   //green
Serial.begin(2000000);
}

void loop() {
  Pot_ADU = analogRead(pinPot);
Serial.println(analogRead(pinPot));
  analogWrite(pinRed, Pot_ADU / 4);
  analogWrite(pinBlue, 255-Pot_ADU / 4);
}
```

This sketch will read the voltage on the pot, plot it to the serial link and convert this number into a color. A blue, cool, low temperature color means a low voltage, a red, warmer color means a higher voltage.

Try this experiment: How would you encode a voltage into the red and green colors?

3.11 Summary of the commands introduced so far

Command	**Description**
void setup (){ }	This is a function that appears in EVERY sketch. Every command within the brackets will be executed just once
void loop (){ }	This is a function that appears in EVERY sketch. Every command within the brackets will execute over and over again.
`pinMode(13, OUTPUT);`	This command tells the Arduino that we are going to use a specific digital pin as an `OUTPUT`, as distinct from an `INPUT`. We use the pin number to identify the pin we want to setup.

digitalWrite(13, HIGH);	This command controls the output of a digital pin and makes it either a HIGH (logic 1, or 5 V) or a LOW (a logic 0 or a 0 V). Once executed, the pin value will be set to this value.
delay(1000);	This command for tell the Arduino to sit there, twiddling its thumbs, doing nothing for a duration of milliseconds as listed inside the (). In this example, the time interval to wait is 1000 msec = 1 sec.
// or /* */	Everything after these two forward slashes will be ignored by the Arduino sketch. We can use this add comments for our own benefit on any line. For multiple lines add them between the /* and the */ lines.
delayMicroseconds(1000);	Just like the delay() function, this function will force the Arduino to sit there and do nothing, for a time duration equal to the time, in microseconds inside the (). In this examples, 1000 microseconds = 1 msec = 0.001 sec.
Serial.begin(9600);	This command opens up the serial com link with a baud rated inside the (). In this example the baud rate is 9600 baud. The name Serial is an object, the serial link. The .begin is a verb, telling the object to get set up.

`Serial.print("Hello World");`	This command will print characters to the serial communications channel. Everything inside the () will be printed. To print a string, enclose the characters within quotes. After printing, the cursor will be left on the same line.
`Serial.println(" ");`	Does the same thing as the `Serial.print` command, but moves the cursor to the next line after printing the characters.
`int`	We use this to assign a variable name as a new variable. It is place at the beginning of the sketch. We have to assign a variable name to a type of variable. This command creates a variable that is a + or – whole number up to 2^{15} = 32, 767
`long`	This assigns a variable name to a + and – whole number up to 2^31 = 2,147, 483, 647. Use this when we expect to be counting very large number. You can never go wrong making all integer variables Long variable.
`float`	This assigns a variable as a floating-point number, which is any number having a decimal point. Use this command when the variable needs to have a decimal point.
`float` Name[100]	Declares an array using the [] to define the number of elements in the array size. Limited to about 301 elements in the Uno

`for (int i = 1; i <= 10; i++) {`
`  //execute this code if i<=10`
`}`
	This is a loop that causes all the code within the { and } brackets to execute for a certain number of times. Inside the () of the command are three sections, separated by ;. The first sets up the index that will step, and its initial value. The second, sets up the condition. While this is true the loop continues. When it is false, the loop breaks to after the }. The last section increments the index, i, by 1.

`sin(Phase_rad)`	This function returns the value of the sine of the number inside the (), assuming this number is an angle in radians. 2 x π radians = 360 deg.
digitalRead(5)	This command will read the digital value of the pin number inside the (), 5, in this example, and return the value as a 0 or 1 or false or true. Once executed, this command becomes the value it reads.
millis()	This function returns the value of the internal counter which is counting the number of milliseconds since the beginning of the sketch. Nothing is placed inside the (). This is a long integer. Every time it is called, it becomes the current value of milliseconds.

micros()	This function returns the value of the internal timer, which is counting up microseconds since the start of the sketch. The resolution is 4 microseconds. Nothing is placed inside the (). This is a long integer. Every time it is called, it becomes the current value of microseconds.
`while (i>1) {` `}`	This command will cause all the code within the {…} to execute over and over again, as long as the condition inside the (…) is true.
`random(min, max);`	This command returns a random integer value that is between the min value and the (max-1) value. The random number returned is a long integer.
`analogRead(pinNumber);`	This command will read the ADC channel in the (), as A0, A1,…A5, and return the value as an integer in units of ADUs. The resolution is 10-bit or 1023 different levels. It takes 112 usec to perform one analogRead(pinNumber); operation.
`analogWrite(pinNumber, value);`	Controls a PWM signal on selected digital pins which modulates the signal at 490 Hz or 980 Hz. The "value" is an integer from 0 to 255 that controls the duty cycle of the PWM signal.

Chapter 4. Test Your Reflexes with Light Flashes

In this experiment, we will build a simple instrument we can use to measure a subject's response time.

The basic operation is, we generate a stimulus and the subject pushes a button when they perceive it. We measure the time interval between when the stimulus started and when the button was pushed.

In this first series of experiments, the stimulus will be a light flash from an LED. In the second series of experiments, the stimulus will be a buzzer.

If we keep the time when the light stimulus flashes a fixed time after the last button is pushed, it's easy to imagine the subject getting into a rhythm and measuring almost a zero-reaction time.

To avoid this potential problem, we'll have to add a little randomness to the time at which the light flashes.

We'll use the multi-function board to flash the light and allow the user to push the response button.

4.1 Planning the experiment

We have available on the multi-function board, two LEDs, a red one and a blue on. Right below them are two switches, labeled SW1 and SW2.

We can use any combination of these as stimulus and response.

The general plan is to:

1. *Select the LED and the switch.*
2. *Turn on the LED for some period of time and start the timer.*
3. *Stop the timer when the switch is pressed.*
4. *Display the time interval for each test on the serial monitor or the serial plotter.*
5. *Wait some amount of time that has a random component and then start over again*
6. *Perform some number of consecutive tests and then calculate some statistics like the average time, or standard deviation, or trend line as a "learning curve" effect.*

To make this happen we will have to introduce a few new features in the software and hardware and a few new science and electronics principles:

- *addressing the on-board LEDs*
- *using the switches on the multi-function board*
- *a new loop function, While*
- *a new coding feature, the timers*
- *a new coding feature, a random number generator*

4.2 Addressing the LEDs

The Blue LED is connected to digital pin 13 and the red LED to digital pin 12.

We can create two variables to keep track of these as:

```
int pinLED_red = 12
int pinLED_blue = 13;
```

When naming variables, my style is to use the more general term first, and then the specific identifiers last. When appropriate, the last part of the variable name is the units.

In the void setup() function we will need to set the pinMode for these two digital pins as OUTPUT.

4.3 New Hardware: Switches

The two switches are connected to the digital pins D2 and D3. These are highlighted in Figure 4.1. Normally, when not touched, the switches are open. When pushed down and they click, the terminals or end conductors on either end of the switch are connected together with a very low resistance. Releasing the switch opens the circuit between its ends.

Figure 4.1 There are two white switches on the Multi-function board, identified in the circle, connected to digital pins D2 and D3.

To use the switch as an indicator of whether the user, us, is pressing the switch, we need to be able to read the resistance of the switch- is it open (not pressed) or is it closed (pressed)?

To do this, we use a common circuit which turns the open or short of the switch into a HIGH or LOW voltage which can be read by a digitalRead() command. We will use a very valuable trick to do this.

The circuit is shown in Figure 4.2.

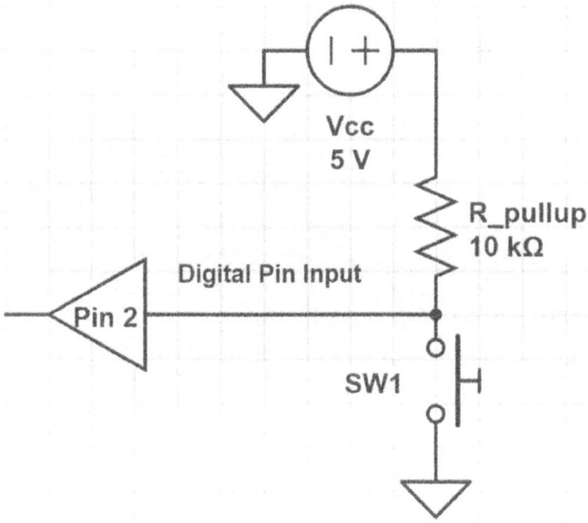

Figure 4.2 Simple circuit that turns the open or closed switch into a HIGH or LOW voltage.

The input to the digital pin is connected to a resistor which is connected to the + 5 V rail. This resistor is sometimes called a pullup resistor, as it pulls the line up, or HIGH, when nothing else is connected to the line.

When the switch is open, it is as though the resistor directly connects the pin input to 5 V and the pin input is read as a HIGH. We refer to this condition as the pin is pulled HIGH.

When the switch is pressed, the switch connects the digital pin input to ground, and the digital pin input is read as a LOW.

When the switch is closed, the current through the resistor, drawn from the 5 V rail, is 5 V/10k Ohms = 0.5 mA, a minimal amount of current.

This is precisely the circuit used on the multi-function board. On the board is a 10k resistor connecting the switch to 5 V. The other end of the switch is connected to ground.

When the switch is not pressed, the inputs on pins D2 and D3 read HIGH. When one of the switches is pressed, it connects the input of the pin to ground through the switch. The pin sees a digital LOW.

The result is a little counter intuitive. When the switch is not pressed, the value read on the digital input is HIGH. When the switch is pressed, the output is LOW.

It would be nice to invert this. I find it more intuitive to read a LOW when the switch is not pressed (a false) and a HIGH when the switch is pressed (a true).

We make this inversion with a simple command.

4.4 New Code: Using the "!" Not command to Turn a 0 into a 1 and a 1 into a 0

When we read a digital input, we can describe the value returned in three different ways, all equivalent:

- *As a 0 and a 1 integer*
- *As a LOW and a HIGH*
- *As a logical false or true*

If we assign an integer to the value read by the digitalWrite() command, the integer value will be a 0 or a 1.

We could do some arithmetic to convert the 0 into a 1 or vis versa.

Alternatively, there is a simple command built into the Arduino IDE to convert a logical 0 into a logical 1 or a true into a false, or vis versa. The command is the NOT command, we invoke with the exclamation point, "!".

We use this command like this. If the SW1 setting is not pressed, the digital value read will be a HIGH or 1 or true. We turn it into a LOW or digital 0 or false with:

int i1 = !digitalRead(pinSW1)

The value of the variable i1 will be 0 (false) when the switch is not pressed and 1 (true) when the switch is pressed. This is exactly how I like to see it. When nothing is happening, you read a 0. When something happens, the switch is pressed, you read a 1.

Try this experiment: To test this property, we can record the high or low value, assign it a number and plot it on the Serial Plotter in real time. We can show the switch position on a graph as we manipulate it.

Think about how you would implement this feature. Try writing the code to display the switch position as a number and plot it in real time.

Keep in mind that if the number plotted is 0 and 1, it will be plotted on a scale of +/-6 full scale, so will not be very large on the screen.

After you have tried this experiment, take a look at my code below:

```
// exp 4 testing reflexes
int pinLED_red = 12;
int pinLED_blue = 13;
int pinSW1 = 2;
int pinSW2 = 3;

void setup() {
  pinMode(pinLED_blue, OUTPUT);
  pinMode(pinLED_red, OUTPUT);
  pinMode(pinSW1, INPUT);
  pinMode(pinSW2, INPUT);
  Serial.begin(2000000);
}
void loop() {
  Serial.println(100 * !digitalRead(pinSW1));
```

```
  delay(50);
}
```

If you run this code and open the serial monitor, you will see either 0 printed or 100 printed. The data comes out very fast. Likewise, on the plotter, its rather boring, just a bunch of straight lines at a value of either 0 or 100.

I added a delay function of 50 msec between points just to slow down the plotting to see some patterns. In Figure 4.3, I pressed the switch for different durations which showed up as pressed states with a plotted value of 100, and not pressed states, with a value of 0.

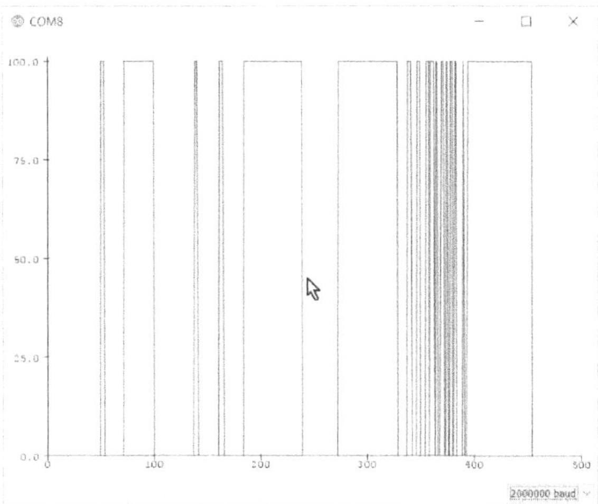

Figure 4.3 The output of the serial plotter showing multiple presses of the switch with long presses and short presses, with a delay of 50 msec between points.

This makes more sense to me. The low value is switch not-pressed and the high value is switch-pressed.

In this example, the delay between samples is 50 msec. With a total of 500 point across the plotter, the total time interval displayed is 500 points x 0.05 sec/point = 25 seconds.

4.5 New Code: timers

The Arduino IDE has a few built-in features to help us measure the passage of time. These are generally called *timers*.

When the Arduino starts the execution of a sketch it starts an internal clock ticking at the clock frequency of 16 MHz. This is a tick every 1/16 MHz = 62.5 nanoseconds. This is a really short period of time.

Inside the Arduino is a counter that, instead of counting each individual clock tick, counts up 64 clock ticks at a time and increments a counter.

With a little arithmetic, we see that 64 ticks x 0.0625 microseconds/tick is really 4 microseconds. We usually abbreviate this as 4 usec.

This means the internal timer of the Arduino counts how many ticks since the start of the sketch in increments of 4 usec. It records the time interval since the start of the sketch in both microseconds and milliseconds.

The time since the start of the sketch, in units of microseconds, is stored in a register as an unsigned long integer. Its value can be read at any instant with the command, micros().

It is important to note that while the value of the time counter is in units of usec, its resolution is only 4 usec. We cannot measure a time interval smaller than 4 usec, or to finer steps than 4 usec.

The time since the start of the sketch, in units of milliseconds, is stored in a register as an unsigned long integer. Its value can be read at any instant with the command, millis().

As an unsigned long integer, the longest time we can measure with the micros() timer is 4,294,967,294 usec. This is 4,294 seconds, or about 70 minutes.

If we use the millis() time, we could measure a time interval as large as 4,294,967,295 milliseconds. This number of milliseconds corresponds to

4,294,967,295 milliseconds =

4,294,967,295 msec x 1 sec/1000 msec = 4,294,967 seconds.

4,294,967 seconds x 1 hour/3600 sec = 1193 hours

1193 hr/24 hr = 49 days

A millisecond is a really short amount of time. We can't directly sense a time interval as short as a millisecond. But, when we measure things, we can use instruments, like an Arduino, to measure and sense time intervals as short as a millisecond and even shorter.

We will use these time meters to measure how long it takes to complete the 500 digital read measurements and print them to the serial monitor at 2,000,000 baud.

One approach is to use a variable to record the time from the microsecond timer at the start of the interval, and then subtract this initial value from the timer counter at the end of the interval. The difference is the interval in microseconds.

4.6 Timing any operation

This technique is a powerful method of measuring the time interval for any operation. We can use it to measure the execution time for operations like:

- *Measuring a voltage on the analog channel*
- *Printing a number to the serial link at different baud rates*
- *Measuring the time to execute a digitalWrite command*
- *Measuring the time to execute a digitalRead command*
- *And others.*

The algorithm will be:

- *Start the timer.*
- *Use a for loop to cycle through n identical, repeating operations*
- *Stop the counter after completing the n operations*
- *We've counted the total time for n operations, so divide the total time by n to get the time per operation.*
- *Print this number out to view it*
- *Repeat to check reproducibility*

Try this experiment: Measure the time it takes to take a reading on the analog point using the analogRead() command.

If you get stuck, here is my sketch:

```
long npts_ave = 1000;
long iTime0_usec;
float TimeX_usec;
long dummy;

void setup() {
  Serial.begin(2000000);
}
void loop() {
  iTime0_usec = micros();
  for (int i = 1; i <= npts_ave; i++) {
    dummy = analogRead(A0);
  }
  TimeX_usec = (micros() - iTime0_usec) / (1.0 * npts_ave);
  Serial.println(TimeX_usec);
}
```

On my Arduino, it takes about 112 usec = 0.000112 sec to perform one ADC reading. This means the sample rate is about 1/0.000112 Hz = 8.928 kHz, almost 9 kHz.

Try these experiments:

What is the execution time of printing 1 character, 10 characters, 50 characters, and at a baud rate of 9600 and 2000000.

How fast can you read a digital pin input?

How fast can you turn off and on a digital pin?

4.7 New Code: The While statement

As part of our reflex timer experiment, we need to continually monitor the switch, and when it is pressed, start a series of operations.

As is often the case, especially in creative activities, there are more than one way of accomplishing this action.

This sort of operation, changing the flow of the code when a button is switched, could be done with an *interrupt* routine. This is a perfectly fine way of implementing this function. It just is a little advanced.

Instead, we will take a simpler approach and introduce a new function, the *While command.* It is a command that controls the flow of the code execution. It's syntax, as listed in the references, is:

```
var = 0;

while (var < 200) {

  // do something repetitive 200 times

  var++;

}
```

The *while command* will loop continuously, executing the code within the curly brackets, {…}, as long as the conditional inside the () is true. As soon as the conditional is false, the flow of code drops to after the ending curly bracket, }.

The idea is, when we start looking to see if the switch has been pressed, we keep reading the switch setting over and over again, as long as the switch has not been pressed.

Remember the switch values:

- *If it is not being pressed, it is reading a HIGH, or a true*
- *If it is being pressed, it is reading a LOW or a false.*

When we first see it pressed, we stop looking at the switch and start executing the code that follows.

This is a simple conditional. We will use it in a clever way. While the switch is not pressed, reading a true, we want to sit there, just repeating the measurement, testing the switch. When the switch is pressed, we want to get out of the while loop.

Try this experiment: How would you use the while statement to control the code to stay in the loop while the switch is not pressed, but get out of the loop when the switch is pressed? When you detect the switch pressed, returning a logical false, flash the blue LED.

Here is a hint: When the switch is not pressed, we want a true statement, so the while statement just sits there talking to itself, continually testing the switch.

After you have tried this, take a look at my code. this is just the stuff needed inside the void loop (). Before this line is all the setup code.

At the beginning of the loop, we start monitoring the switch. While the digitalRead () value is true, a digital 1, meaning the switch is not pressed, the while loop executes, and it sits there going round and round, retesting the digital pin.

```
int pinSW1=2;
```

```
int pinLED_blue=13;

void setup() {
  // put your setup code here, to run once:
}

void loop() {
  while (digitalRead(pinSW1)) {}
  digitalWrite(pinLED_blue, HIGH);
  delay(100);
  digitalWrite(pinLED_blue, LOW);
}
```

As soon as the digitalRead value is false, meaning the switch is pressed, the code execution moves out of the while loop to the next line after the curly brackets and flashes the LED.

Now we are ready to write the full sketch to measure the time between turning the light on and seeing the switch closed.

Try this experiment: How would you write the code to:

1. *turn on the LED*
2. *read the timer*
3. *read the switch*
4. *when the switch is pressed, read the current time*
5. *calculate the reflex time*
6. *print out the time*
7. *start over again*

Spend some time to work through the details and test out the results.

If you get stuck, take a look at my code:

```
// exp 4 testing reflexes
```

```
////change these variables///////
int npts = 10; // the number of readings per run
int iDelay_msec = 1000;

///fixed variables///////
int pinLED_red = 12;
int pinLED_blue = 13;
int pinSW1 = 2;
int pinSW2 = 3;
long iTime0_msec;
long iTime1_msec;
float TimeInterval_msec;

void setup() {
  pinMode(pinLED_blue, OUTPUT);
  pinMode(pinLED_red, OUTPUT);
  pinMode(pinSW1, INPUT);
  pinMode(pinSW2, INPUT);
  Serial.begin(2000000);
}
void loop() {
  for (int i = 1; i <= npts; i++) {
    digitalWrite(pinLED_blue, HIGH);
    iTime0_msec = millis();

    while (digitalRead(pinSW1)) {}

    iTime1_msec = millis();
    TimeInterval_msec = iTime1_msec - iTime0_msec;
    Serial.println(TimeInterval_msec);
    digitalWrite(pinLED_blue, LOW);
    delay(iDelay_msec);
  }
  delay(10000);
}
```

4.8 Learning the pattern

The core of the sketch to test and record our reflexes is ready. There are just a few slight modifications to optimize the experiment.

Initially, we are waiting a fixed time after completing one test before the LED flashes again. If we use this code, we may be introducing a small artifact.

We tend to learn repetitive patterns and adapt. If the user learns the pattern of when to anticipate the next flash, their reaction time might get better as they practice these trials.

This was certainly the case when I played with this sketch to test my reaction time. Figure 4.4 is the recording of ten trials. My reaction time got shorter during the test.

```
COM4

274.00
189.00
136.00
168.00
174.00
149.00
132.00
154.00
175.00
62.00
```

Figure 4.4. The ten recordings of my reaction time with a fixed time interval between pushes. I learned quickly to anticipate the light flash.

Try this experiment: This would be a really interesting behavior to test. Use a fixed time between the end of the last trial and when the next light flashes. Plot the reaction time of the test subject vs trial number on the Serial Plotter. Do you see the reaction time decrease with experience as the pattern is learned?

4.9 New code: random numbers

To avoid this potential source of bias, we should add a little randomness to the time between trials, so it is harder to guess. The way we will do this is by using a *random number generator.*

The random() function will generate "pseudo random" numbers. They are random enough for our purposes. The random number generator and using it to plot random walk paths was introduced in Arduinos Without Tears.

The syntax of the function is

```
i1=random(min, max);
```

Every time this code is executed the value of i1 would be a different random number between the minimum value and the max value, not inclusive of the max value. It will return a long integer.

If we want a random number between 0 and 1000, we would use random(0, 1001). This can be shortened to random(1001).

Try this experiment: How would you implement the delay between tests with a base value of 1000 msec plus a random number of msec between 0 to 1000 msec?

We should conduct trials in groups of some number like 10 or twenty. Within each group of trials, we can calculate the average value at the end of the trials.

To calculate the average, we add up all the values and divide by the number of trials in each group.

Finally, we should add a short delay at the beginning of the trial. When we open the Serial Monitor, a reset signal is sent to the Arduino to start the sketch from the beginning. The delay at the start will give you time to get ready after we start the sketch.

Try this experiment: Write the complete code that would test your reflexes with the delay at the beginning, the random delay and the average.

After you have had a chance to try your hand at creating this code, take a look at how I implemented it. Remember, there are many right ways to implement this code.

4.10 Sketch: Testing your Reflexes

```
// exp 4 testing reflexes
////change these variables///////
int npts = 10; // the number of readings per run

///fixed variables///////
int pinLED_red = 12;
int pinLED_blue = 13;
int pinSW1 = 2;
int pinSW2 = 3;
long iTime0_msec;
long iTime1_msec;
long iTimeInterval_msec;
float TimeAve_msec;

void setup() {
  pinMode(pinLED_blue, OUTPUT);
  pinMode(pinLED_red, OUTPUT);
  pinMode(pinSW1, INPUT);
  pinMode(pinSW2, INPUT);
  Serial.begin(2000000);
}
void loop() {
  TimeAve_msec = 0.0;
  Serial.println("Get ready to begin");
  delay(3000);
  for (int i = 1; i <= npts; i++) {
    digitalWrite(pinLED_blue, HIGH);
```

```
    iTime0_msec = millis();
    while (digitalRead(pinSW1)) {}
    iTime1_msec = millis();
    iTimeInterval_msec = iTime1_msec - iTime0_msec;
    TimeAve_msec = TimeAve_msec + iTimeInterval_msec;
    Serial.println(iTimeInterval_msec);
    digitalWrite(pinLED_blue, LOW);
    delay(1000 + random(1000));
  }
  TimeAve_msec = TimeAve_msec / npts;
  Serial.print("Average reaction time is: ");
  Serial.print(TimeAve_msec); Serial.println(" msec");
  Serial.println("");
  Serial.println("");
  Serial.println("");
  delay(10000);
}
```

When this is executed, I pressed the switch when the blue light flashed on. Figure 4.5 shows the result.

```
COM5

Get ready to begin
222
191
200
189
194
214
196
176
166
198
Average reaction time is: 194.60 msec
```

Figure 4.5 An example of the output display of my reaction times to seeing the blue light flash on. My reflex time is about 195 msec.

This is the basic code you need to perform a variety of experiments.

4.11 A series of reaction time experiments

Using this code as the starting place, here are some cool experiments to try which give us insight into how the input from sensors are wired in your brain to your fingers, as actuators.

Try some of these experiments:

1. *Does your reaction time depend on whether you see a blue light flash or a red-light flash?*

2. *In first round of experiments, we kept the light on until the switch is pushed. Suppose we use a pulse which is on for a time shorter than our reaction time, like 150 msec, or shorter.*

3. *Does your reaction time increase or decrease when a pulse is used? How short a pulse can we respond to? Do we push the switch on the turn-on of the light or the turn-off of the light?*

4. *In the first round of experiments, we looked at the light with both eyes and pushed the switch with one hand. Suppose we use a patch over one eye, so we only see the light with the other eye.*

5. *Is there a different reaction time, if we see the light with our right eye and push the button with our right hand, or left hand? This is a test of our dominant hand.*

6. *Is there a different reaction time, if we see the light with our left eye and push the button with our right hand, or left hand? This is a test of our dominant eye*

7. *In the early experiment, we used a random delay between each test. Does our reaction time change if we make the delay between flashes longer or shorter?*

8. *In the early experiment, we used a random delay between each test. Does our reaction time change if we make the delay between flashes exactly the same amount of time? Do we learn*

the delay and anticipate the flash, decreasing our reaction time?

9. *In the early experiments, we used one LED and one switch. Suppose we select the red or blue LED at random and use just the one switch.*

10. *Does our reaction time depend on which LED flashes and whether it is adjacent to the switch we are pressing?*

11. *In the early experiments, we used one LED and one switch. Suppose we select the red or blue LED at random and use just two switches. If the blue LED flashes, we have to press the switch under the blue LED. If the red LED flashes, we have to press the switch under the red LED.*

12. *How does the reaction time of one person vary with others? Is there a relationship between reaction time and the amount of time per week you spend playing games?*

4.12 Summary of the commands introduced so far

Command	**Description**

void setup (){
 	
}
	This is a function that appears in EVERY sketch. Every command within the brackets will be executed just once

void loop (){
 	
}
	This is a function that appears in EVERY sketch. Every command within the brackets will execute over and over again.

`pinMode(13, OUTPUT);`	This command tells the Arduino that we are going to use a specific digital pin as an `OUTPUT`, as distinct from an `INPUT`. We use the pin number to identify the pin we want to setup.
`digitalWrite(13, HIGH);`	This command controls the output of a digital pin and makes it either a `HIGH` (logic 1, or 5 V) or a `LOW` (a logic 0 or a 0 V). Once executed, the pin value will be set to this value.
`delay(1000);`	This command for tell the Arduino to sit there, twiddling its thumbs, doing nothing for a duration of milliseconds as listed inside the (). In this example, the time interval to wait is 1000 msec = 1 sec.
// or /* */	Everything after these two forward slashes will be ignored by the Arduino sketch. We can use this add comments for our own benefit on any line. For multiple lines add them between the /* and the */ lines.
`delayMicroseconds(1000);`	Just like the `delay()` function, this function will force the Arduino to sit there and do nothing, for a time duration equal to the time, in microseconds inside the (). In this examples, 1000 microseconds – 1 msec = 0.001 sec.
`Serial.begin(9600);`	This command opens up the serial com link with a baud rated inside the (). In this example the baud rate is 9600 baud. The name `Serial` is an object, the serial link. The `.begin` is a verb, telling the object to get set up.

`Serial.print("Hello World");`	This command will print characters to the serial communications channel. Everything inside the () will be printed. To print a string, enclose the characters within quotes. After printing, the cursor will be left on the same line.
`Serial.println(" ");`	Does the same thing as the `Serial.print` command, but moves the cursor to the next line after printing the characters.
`int`	We use this to assign a variable name as a new variable. It is place at the beginning of the sketch. We have to assign a variable name to a type of variable. This command creates a variable that is a + or – whole number up to 2^{15} = 32, 767
`long`	This assigns a variable name to a + and – whole number up to 2^31 = 2,147, 483, 647. Use this when we expect to be counting very large number. You can never go wrong making all integer variables Long variable.
`float`	This assigns a variable as a floating-point number, which is any number having a decimal point. Use this command when the variable needs to have a decimal point.

`for (int i = 1; i <= 10; i++) {`
`  //execute this code if i<=10`
`}`
	This is a loop that causes all the code within the { and } brackets to execute for a certain number of times. Inside the () of the command are three sections, separated by ;. The first sets up the index that will step, and its initial value. The second, sets up the condition. While this is true the loop continues. When it is false, the loop breaks to after the }. The last section increments the index, i, by 1.

`sin(Phase_rad)`	This function returns the value of the sine of the number inside the (), assuming this number is an angle in radians. 2 x π radians = 360 deg.
digitalRead(5)	This command will read the digital value of the pin number inside the (), 5, in this example, and return the value as a 0 or 1 or false or true. Once executed, this command becomes the value it reads.
millis()	This function returns the value of the internal counter which is counting the number of milliseconds since the beginning of the sketch. Nothing is placed inside the (). This is a long integer. Every time it is called, it becomes the current value of milliseconds.
micros()	This function returns the value of the internal timer, which is counting up microseconds since the start of the sketch. The resolution is 4 microseconds. Nothing is placed inside the (). This is a long integer. Every time it is called, it becomes the current value of microseconds.

`while (i>1) {` `}`	This command will cause all the code within the {…} to execute over and over again, as long as the condition inside the (…) is true.
`random(min, max);`	This command returns a random integer value that is between the min value and the (max-1) value. The random number returned is a long integer.

Chapter 5. Test Your Reflexes with a Buzzer

In the last experiment, we used a flashing LED light as the stimulus. Is there any difference in our reaction time, if the stimulus is an audible buzz? We can test this.

We will implement the same code as before and perform the same measurements as before but using a buzzer as the stimulus.

In addition, we will be using a new piece of hardware. Our first step is to explore some of its features and the range of what it can do by *reverse engineering* its properties. Using simple code to manipulate it, we will *hack into it* and explore everything it can do.

5.1 New Hardware: The buzzer

There are two types of buzzers, ones for which you apply a DC voltage and it self-oscillates, and ones which only click when the signal to it changes from an off to on or an on to off. It requires a pulsed signal and vibrates at the applied pulse frequency.

The buzzer in the Multi-function board is the first type. It self-oscillates when you apply a DC voltage of 5 V. All we have to do is turn on the digital HIGH and it buzzes.

WARNING- this buzzer has an obnoxious buzz. Be prepared to unplug the power or turn on a HIGH initially for a short period of time

The large black buzzer on this multi-function board is shown in Figure 5.1.

Figure 5.1 The buzzer on the Multi-function board is connected to digital pin D5. Apply a DC voltage on D5 and the buzzer blasts away as long as the voltage is applied.

It is connected to digital pin 5. It only buzzes when a digital HIGH is applied to pin 5. The buzzer clicks at a specific rate of roughly 300 Hz. It self-oscillates and the oscillation frequency cannot be adjusted.

Just to get a feel for using the buzzer, we can try modulating the buzzer on and off for some amount of time.

We will use a simple pattern with the on-time and off-time we change independently.

Try this experiment: Create the code to turn the buzzer on for a second, then off for a second, and repeat this pattern. Just the description should sound very familiar. After all, this is just Blink.

Try this experiment: When you play the buzzer, you may find it is really loud and obnoxious. You probably don't want it blasting away and repeating for very long. Structure your code so that the sound only plays for a few repeat cycles and then it turns itself off.

And, while you are at it, write your sketch so it is parameterized. We want to be able to change the on-time, the off-time and the number of cycles that are played before it turns off.

This idea of parameterizing your code is so important. The more clearly we can see where we want to go in an experiment, the better we can structure the code for flexibility.

As a __Best Design Practice__, always try to think about how to structure your code with variables that can be set at the beginning of the sketch and give you the most flexibility for changing terms and exploring a range of behaviors.

After you have tried this experiment, take a look at my code:

```
int pinBuzz = 5;
int nCycles = 5; // the number of cycles to play
long iTimeOn_msec = 1000;
long iTimeOff_msec = 1000;

void setup() {
  pinMode(pinBuzz, OUTPUT);
  for (int i = 1; i <= nCycles; i++) {
    digitalWrite(pinBuzz, HIGH);
    delay(iTimeOn_msec);
    digitalWrite(pinBuzz, LOW);
    delay(iTimeOff_msec);
  }
}
void loop() {
}
```

Like all coding experiments, there are many ways of accomplishing the same function. I wanted the buzzer to repeat for only a few cycles, so I used a *for loop*. I wanted the buzzer to self-terminate after some number of cycles, so I put the code in the `setup` () function. This will execute only once.

How did you implement these features?

> *Just remember that EVERY sketch needs to have both a void setup() AND a void loop() function. Even if there is no code in the section, be sure to keep the void loop() line in your sketch.*

You can literally copy this code from this eBook and paste it into a blank sketch, replacing what is there.

> *Of course, I always recommend, type in each line of code for all of the examples in this eBook. It will help build muscle memory and help you write your own code.*

5.2 Experiment: testing reflexes with the buzzer

Now we are ready to replace the reflex tester with the buzzer as an option.

Try this experiment. We can literally just replace the LED pin control with the buzzer. What would your modified sketch look like? Give it a try before you look at my sketch below.

Here is how I took the reflex tester and added in the buzzer.

```
// exp 4 testing reflexes with buzzer
////change these variables///////
int npts = 10; // the number of readings per run

///fixed variables///////
int pinLED_red = 12;
int pinLED_blue = 13;
int pinBuzz = 5; //changed this
int pinSW1 = 2;
int pinSW2 = 3;
long iTime0_msec;
long iTime1_msec;
```

```
long iTimeInterval_msec;
float TimeAve_msec;

void setup() {
  pinMode(pinLED_blue, OUTPUT);
  pinMode(pinLED_red, OUTPUT);
  pinMode(pinBuzz, OUTPUT); //changed this
  pinMode(pinSW1, INPUT);
  pinMode(pinSW2, INPUT);
  Serial.begin(2000000);
}
void loop() {
  TimeAve_msec = 0.0;
  Serial.println("Get ready to begin");
  delay(3000);
  for (int i = 1; i <= npts; i++) {
    digitalWrite(pinBuzz, HIGH);  //changed this
    iTime0_msec = millis();
    while (digitalRead(pinSW1)) {}
    iTime1_msec = millis();
    iTimeInterval_msec = iTime1_msec - iTime0_msec;
    TimeAve_msec = TimeAve_msec + iTimeInterval_msec;
    Serial.println(iTimeInterval_msec);
    digitalWrite(pinBuzz, LOW);  //changed this
    delay(1000 + random(1000));
  }
  TimeAve_msec = TimeAve_msec / npts;
  Serial.print("Average reaction time is: ");
  Serial.print(TimeAve_msec); Serial.println(" msec");
  Serial.println("");
  Serial.println("");
  Serial.println("");
  delay(10000);
}
```

There were literally only four lines of code that needed to be changed to use the buzzer as the stimulus.

Now we have three options for the stimulus and two options for the response.

Since we have some experience at thinking about parameterizing code to make it flexible, modify this sketch so that we select the stimulus and the response pins at the beginning. Then we can use just one sketch to explore the impact on reflect time on a specific color LED or a buzzer and which buzzer position as the response

Try this experiment. Write your code that parameterizes the stimulus pin and the response pin. After you have given this a try, take a look at my sketch.

5.3 Sketch: Testing your reflexes with a buzzer stimulus

```
// exp 4 testing reflexes with LED or Buzzer
////change these variables///////
int npts = 10; // the number of readings per run
int pinStim = 12; // 13-blue LED, 12-red LED, 5-buzzer
int pinResp = 2; // 2 for SW1, 3 for SW2

///fixed variables///////
long iTime0_msec;
long iTime1_msec;
long iTimeInterval_msec;
float TimeAve_msec;

void setup() {
  pinMode(pinStim, OUTPUT);
  pinMode(pinResp, INPUT);
  Serial.begin(2000000);
}
void loop() {
  TimeAve_msec = 0.0;
  Serial.println("Get ready to begin");
  delay(3000);
  for (int i = 1; i <= npts; i++) {
    digitalWrite(pinStim, HIGH);
    iTime0_msec = millis();
    while (digitalRead(pinResp)) {}
    iTime1_msec = millis();
    iTimeInterval_msec = iTime1_msec - iTime0_msec;
    TimeAve_msec = TimeAve_msec + iTimeInterval_msec;
    Serial.println(iTimeInterval_msec);
    digitalWrite(pinStim, LOW);
    delay(1000 + random(1000));
  }
  TimeAve_msec = TimeAve_msec / npts;
  Serial.print("Average reaction time is: ");
  Serial.print(TimeAve_msec); Serial.println(" msec");
  Serial.println("");
  Serial.println("");
  Serial.println("");
```

```
  delay(10000);
}
```

One of the advantages of using parameterized code is that sometimes it requires fewer lines of code. This is now compact.

We are even positioned so that if we find another device to use as a stimulus, like the three-color LED, or a response, like the photo-resistor, we literally just add it in as an optional pin and are ready to test it in a few seconds.

Try this experiment: Now that we implemented the sketch with the buzzer, give it a try. See if your reaction time is decreased with the audible tone than with the light flash. Do we react faster from a sound stimulus than visual stimulus? This is now a testable experiment.

5.4 Summary of the commands introduced so far

Command	Description

void setup (){
 	
}
	This is a function that appears in EVERY sketch. Every command within the brackets will be executed just once

void loop (){
 	
}
	This is a function that appears in EVERY sketch. Every command within the brackets will execute over and over again.

pinMode(13, OUTPUT);	This command tells the Arduino that we are going to use a specific digital pin as an OUTPUT, as distinct from an INPUT. We use the pin number to identify the pin we want to setup.

`digitalWrite(13, HIGH);`	This command controls the output of a digital pin and makes it either a `HIGH` (logic 1, or 5 V) or a `LOW` (a logic 0 or a 0 V). Once executed, the pin value will be set to this value.
`delay(1000);`	This command for tell the Arduino to sit there, twiddling its thumbs, doing nothing for a duration of milliseconds as listed inside the (). In this example, the time interval to wait is 1000 msec = 1 sec.
// or /* */	Everything after these two forward slashes will be ignored by the Arduino sketch. We can use this add comments for our own benefit on any line. For multiple lines add them between the /* and the */ lines.
delayMicroseconds(1000);	Just like the delay() function, this function will force the Arduino to sit there and do nothing, for a time duration equal to the time, in microseconds inside the (). In this examples, 1000 microseconds = 1 msec = 0.001 sec.
`Serial.begin(9600);`	This command opens up the serial com link with a baud rated inside the (). In this example the baud rate is 9600 baud. The name `Serial` is an object, the serial link. The `.begin` is a verb, telling the object to get set up.

`Serial.print("Hello World");`	This command will print characters to the serial communications channel. Everything inside the () will be printed. To print a string, enclose the characters within quotes. After printing, the cursor will be left on the same line.
`Serial.println(" ");`	Does the same thing as the `Serial.print` command, but moves the cursor to the next line after printing the characters.
`int`	We use this to assign a variable name as a new variable. It is place at the beginning of the sketch. We have to assign a variable name to a type of variable. This command creates a variable that is a + or – whole number up to 2^{15} = 32, 767
`long`	This assigns a variable name to a + and – whole number up to 2^31 = 2,147, 483, 647. Use this when we expect to be counting very large number. You can never go wrong making all integer variables Long variable.
`float`	This assigns a variable as a floating-point number, which is any number having a decimal point. Use this command when the variable needs to have a decimal point.

`for (int i = 1; i <= 10; i++) {`
`//execute this code if i<=10`
`}`
	This is a loop that causes all the code within the { and } brackets to execute for a certain number of times. Inside the () of the command are three sections, separated by ;. The first sets up the index that will step, and its initial value. The second, sets up the condition. While this is true the loop continues. When it is false, the loop breaks to after the }. The last section increments the index, i, by 1.

digitalRead(5)	This command will read the digital value of the pin number inside the (), 5, in this example, and return the value as a 0 or 1 or false or true. Once executed, this command becomes the value it reads.
millis()	This function returns the value of the internal counter which is counting the number of milliseconds since the beginning of the sketch. Nothing is placed inside the (). This is a long integer. Every time it is called, it becomes the current value of milliseconds.
micros()	This function returns the value of the internal timer, which is counting up microseconds since the start of the sketch. The resolution is 4 microseconds. Nothing is placed inside the (). This is a long integer. Every time it is called, it becomes the current value of microseconds.

`while (i>1) {` `}`	This command will cause all the code within the {…} to execute over and over again, as long as the condition inside the (…) is true.
`random(min, max);`	This command returns a random integer value that is between the min value and the (max-1) value. The random number returned is a long integer.

Chapter 6. Calibrate Your Perception of the Passage of Time

One thing I noticed playing with the simple buzzer sketch is that my perception of the duration of a second was not well calibrated.

The buzzer was on for exactly 1 second. The accuracy of the time interval from the Arduino is better than 1%. Yet, I perceived the on-time of the buzzer to be longer than 1 second.

Did you notice the same sensation? This sketch is a great way to calibrate your sense of the passage of time.

Try these experiments:

Is your perception of the passage of 1 second well calibrated?

Use an on-time of 1 second for the buzzer. Does the time the buzzer is on really feel like 1 second? Try 1/2 a second or 2 seconds. Is the on-time what you would have expected as this amount of time.

Try these experiments:

1. *As an alternative experiment, turn the buzzer on and push the button when you perceive 1 second or 2 seconds or 3 seconds have passed.*

2. *Compare your perceived passage of time with the actual amount of time.*

3. *Does the type of stimulus affect your perceived passage of time? If you use an obnoxious stimulus, like the buzzer, do you underestimate the time passage, hoping the buzzer will shut off sooner?*

4. *If the stimulus is a red or blue LED, do you perceive the passage of time differently, depending on whether red or blue is your favorite color?*

5. *Try testing other people. Set the on-time for a fixed period and ask the subject how long they perceive the on-time to be. Try each experiment with a test subject.*

6.1 What it means to do science

These sorts of experiments are examples of what it means to ***do science***.

- *We make an observation that is unexpected.*
- *We think of a possible explanation, (an hypothesis), stated in a way we can test.*
- *We plan an experiment to test the idea.*
- *We conduct the experiments and collect measurements.*
- *We analyze the measured data and extract a few useful pieces of information that parameterizes the information.*
- *We interpret the information to analyze our hypothesis. If the data supports our hypothesis, we might elevate the hypothesis to the next level, as a theory. Or, we might consider other, alternative explanations and consider going back to planning other experiments.*
- *We can never prove a theory or explanation is correct.*
- *All we can do is think of experiments to try and evaluate whether our hypothesis is* ***consistent*** *with the results of the experiment.*
- *The more experiments that are consistent with the predictions of our hypothesis, the more confidence we have in it and the more likely we are willing to elevate it to a theory.*

- *When every experiment we can think of doing is consistent with the predictions of the theory, and we are confident we will not find a contradiction, we sometimes elevate the theory to a law.*
- *At every step we want to consider other, alternative explanations and think of experiments that will show the consistency or inconsistency with our hypothesis or theory.*

This is the process we will use over and over again in this eBook and all the books in the Science Experiments with Arduinos series.

6.2 Experiment: Testing your perception of the passage of time

In the previous experiment, we fixed the on-time of the stimulus and observed the on-time, compared with what we expected.

In this series of experiments, we can let the user define the perceived passage of time by pressing the switch after some fixed time interval has passed and record the time.

We use exactly the same code as the reaction time tester. The only difference is, at the beginning of the experiment, we specify to the subject the time interval to measure.

At the end of the perceived time interval, the subject presses the switch. We display the time interval for each trial and calculate the average after some number of trials. This is displayed on the Serial Monitor.

No change in the sketch is required. We are just changing the test protocol and what we call the measurement. We are now measuring the perception of time passage, not reaction time.

With the sketch you can determine if the passage of time depends on the stimulus which is controlled, a blue LED, a red LED or a buzzer.

Try testing for 0.5 sec, 1 sec, 2 sec and 3 sec of time interval. If the subject is willing, try longer intervals.

6.3 Summary of the commands introduced so far

Command	Description

void setup (){
 	
}
	This is a function that appears in EVERY sketch. Every command within the brackets will be executed just once

void loop (){
 	
}
	This is a function that appears in EVERY sketch. Every command within the brackets will execute over and over again.

`pinMode(13, OUTPUT);`	This command tells the Arduino that we are going to use a specific digital pin as an `OUTPUT`, as distinct from an `INPUT`. We use the pin number to identify the pin we want to setup.
`digitalWrite(13, HIGH);`	This command controls the output of a digital pin and makes it either a `HIGH` (logic 1, or 5 V) or a `LOW` (a logic 0 or a 0 V). Once executed, the pin value will be set to this value.
`delay(1000);`	This command for tell the Arduino to sit there, twiddling its thumbs, doing nothing for a duration of milliseconds as listed inside the (). In this example, the time interval to wait is 1000 msec = 1 sec.

// or /* */	Everything after these two forward slashes will be ignored by the Arduino sketch. We can use this add comments for our own benefit on any line. For multiple lines add them between the /* and the */ lines.
delayMicroseconds(1000);	Just like the delay() function, this function will force the Arduino to sit there and do nothing, for a time duration equal to the time, in microseconds inside the (). In this examples, 1000 microseconds = 1 msec = 0.001 sec.
`Serial.begin(9600);`	This command opens up the serial com link with a baud rated inside the (). In this example the baud rate is 9600 baud. The name `Serial` is an object, the serial link. The `.begin` is a verb, telling the object to get set up.
`Serial.print("Hello World");`	This command will print characters to the serial communications channel. Everything inside the () will be printed. To print a string, enclose the characters within quotes. After printing, the cursor will be left on the same line.
`Serial.println(" ");`	Does the same thing as the `Serial.print` command, but moves the cursor to the next line after printing the characters.

`int`	We use this to assign a variable name as a new variable. It is place at the beginning of the sketch. We have to assign a variable name to a type of variable. This command creates a variable that is a + or – whole number up to 2^{15} = 32, 767
`long`	This assigns a variable name to a + and – whole number up to 2^31 = 2,147, 483, 647. Use this when we expect to be counting very large number. You can never go wrong making all integer variables Long variable.
`float`	This assigns a variable as a floating-point number, which is any number having a decimal point. Use this command when the variable needs to have a decimal point.

`for (int i = 1; i <= 10; i++) {`
`  //execute this code if i<=10`
`}`
	This is a loop that causes all the code within the { and } brackets to execute for a certain number of times. Inside the () of the command are three sections, separated by ;. The first sets up the index that will step, and its initial value. The second, sets up the condition. While this is true the loop continues. When it is false, the loop breaks to after the }. The last section increments the index, i, by 1.

`digitalRead(5)`	This command will read the digital value of the pin number inside the (), 5, in this example, and return the value as a 0 or 1 or false or true. Once executed, this command becomes the value it reads.

millis()	This function returns the value of the internal counter which is counting the number of milliseconds since the beginning of the sketch. Nothing is placed inside the (). This is a long integer. Every time it is called, it becomes the current value of milliseconds.
micros()	This function returns the value of the internal timer, which is counting up microseconds since the start of the sketch. The resolution is 4 microseconds. Nothing is placed inside the (). This is a long integer. Every time it is called, it becomes the current value of microseconds.
`while (i>1) {` `}`	This command will cause all the code within the {…} to execute over and over again, as long as the condition inside the (…) is true.
`random(min, max);`	This command returns a random integer value that is between the min value and the (max-1) value. The random number returned is a long integer.

Chapter 7. Data Logging Temperature and Humidity with a Smart Sensor

The multi-function board has a ***smart sensor*** able to measure both temperature and humidity, the DHT11. We call it smart because inside, it does some processing of the sensor signal, converting it into an encoded digital signal and is read using digital commands. This is different than an ***analog*** sensor that outputs an analog voltage which is read by an ADC channel.

The DHT11 can be seen on the multi-function board as the large light blue square with small holes in its surface. It is highlighted in Figure 7.1.

Figure 7.1. The DHT11 smart temperature and humidity sensor.

Rather than reading a voltage on the sensor, we talk to the sensor through a digital interface.

The sensor is manufactured by Aosong for use in air conditioning systems and inside environments. The datasheet can be downloaded here.

This is not the only smart temperature humidity sensor, but it is probably the lowest cost. In low volume, a few units can be purchased for about $0.50 each.

In this experiment, we will read the sensor values, record them, plot them and bring them into excel or another spreadsheet.

7.1 DHT11 smart sensor and its library

The DHT11 is an old-style sensor, not very fast, not very high performance, but very low cost and easy to use.

Every smart sensor communicates using digital signals with the microcontroller. Generally, the language it uses is very specialized and custom to that sensor.

Some smart sensors use an I2C interface, some an SPI interface. These are standard interfaces which the Arduino understands.

The DHT11 uses its own language and transmits its signals to and from the microcontroller using just one digital pin, measured relative to a ground connection. It receives its power from the 5 V power rail of the Arduino. This means there are a minimum of three wires to the DHT11.

Luckily, all the wiring and connections are already handled by the multi-function board. All we have to do is talk to the sensor by writing a little bit of code.

On the multi-function board, the digital pin connecting to the DHT11 is pin D4. The power and ground pins of the DHT11 are also connected to the Arduino's power and ground pins.

With a custom protocol used to communicate between the Arduino and sensor, it sounds like talking to the DHT11 could be very complicated. What makes the communication and control of the smart sensors really easy is the use of special programs called *libraries*.

Libraries are special programs that the Arduino IDE can access which will convert the native language of the sensor to a higher level, simpler language, we can write in our sketch.

Every smart sensor usually has multiple libraries we can use, some easier to figure out than others. The easiest way to find them is to search the vendor we bought the sensor from, or to Google it.

Sometimes we can have the Arduino IDE find the library for us automatically. In the case of the DHT11, there is a simple, easy to use library which you can access right from the Arduino IDE.

Under the menu item *sketch*, find the line item *Include Library*, near the bottom of the list and select it. This item is shown selected in Figure 7.2. This will open up a new menu with a list of many libraries which can be automatically installed in the IDE.

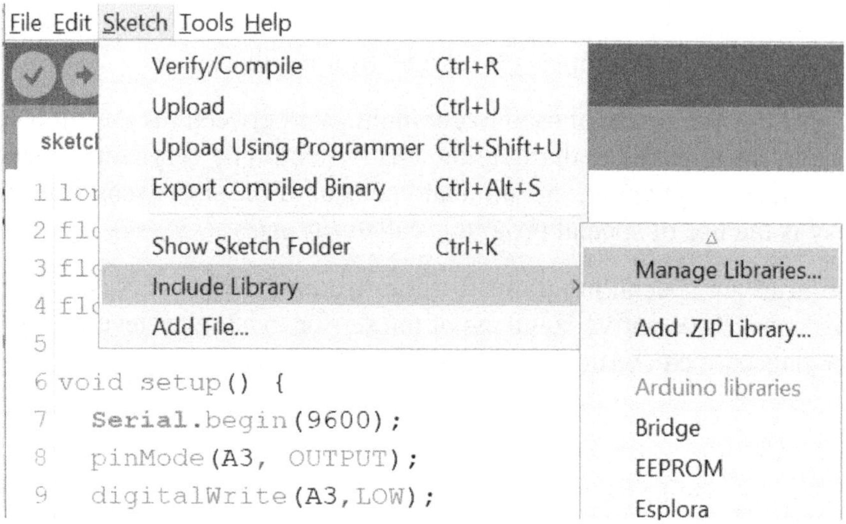

Figure 7.2. The pull-down item Include Library under sketch.

In the search box of this new page, you should type in *DHT11*. When you click on search, you will find a few options, as shown in Figure 7.3.

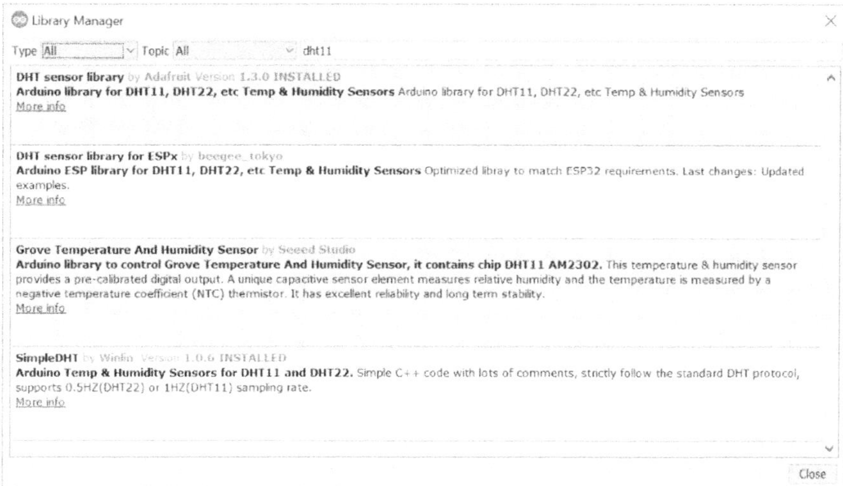

Figure 7.3. Examples of the libraries that appear when searching for the DHT11. Select the Simple DHT library.

While all of these libraries may work, some are easier to use than others. I recommend selecting the last one, labeled as *Simple DHT*. Select this box and you will see an *Install* button on the lower right of the box. Click this button and you are done.

The simplest way of using this library is to run an example and then modify it to meet your needs. From the *file* menu, select *Examples*. You will have to scroll way down to the bottom of the list.

When you installed the SimpleDHT library, it installed a few new example sketches in the example list. The best one to start with is labeled as DHT11 Default. This is shown in **Error! Reference source not found.**.

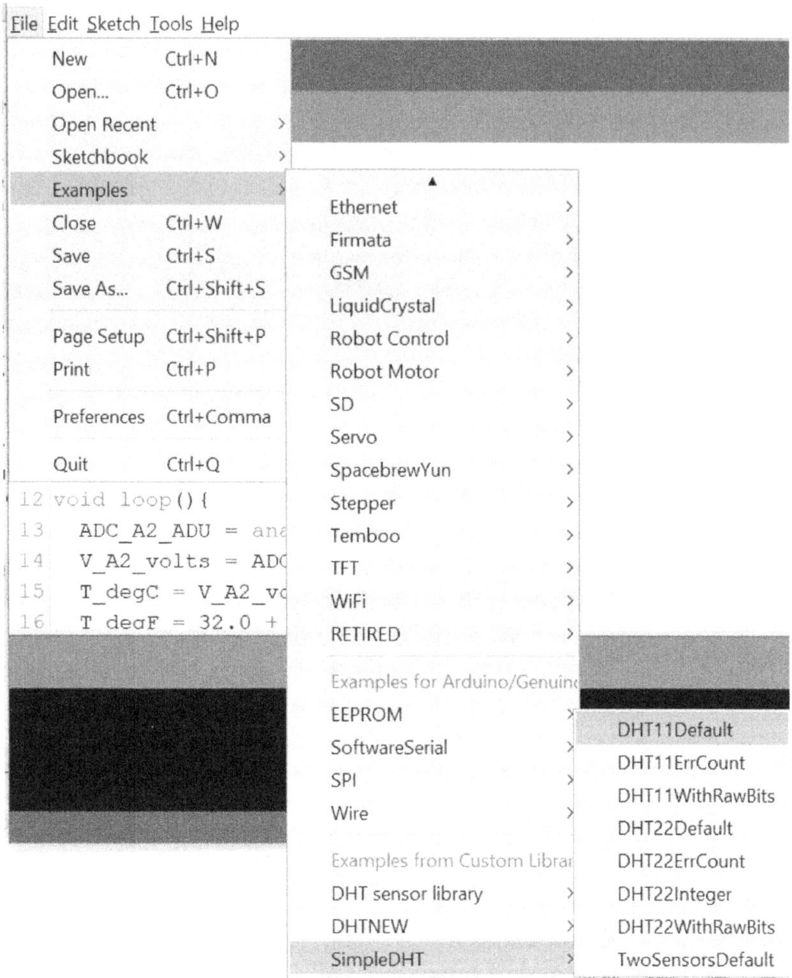

Figure 7.4. To start out, select under examples, and SimpleDHT, the DHT11Default sketch

Selecting this option will open up an example in a new sketch. Before we run it, we need to make an important modification. Take a look at the complete sketch.

There is a lot of error checking and commenting going on in this sketch. The most important change we need to make is the identification of the digital pin the DHT11 data pin connects. In this example sketch, the default pin selected is 2. We need to change this to ***pin 4***, based on the connection on the multi-function board.

I also recommend changing the baud rate to 2000000 in the Serial.begin line.

These are the only changes we need to make. At this point, we can go ahead and test out the sketch. Make sure the correct board and com port are selected. Then click *upload.*

Open up the serial monitor, and you should see the listing of the temperature and humidity. An example is shown in Figure 7.5.

```
=================================
Sample DHT11...
Sample OK: 25 *C, 36 H
=================================
Sample DHT11...
Sample OK: 25 *C, 36 H
=================================
Sample DHT11...
Sample OK: 25 *C, 36 H
=================================
Sample DHT11...
Sample OK: 25 *C, 36 H
=================================
Sample DHT11...
Sample OK: 25 *C, 36 H
```

Figure 7.5 The output on the serial monitor of this simple default sketch.

Now that we have the Arduino talking to the sensor and displaying the results, we can start modifying it to simplify it and do some reverse engineering.

7.2 Modifying the sketch for our experiments

When you look over the sketch, you will notice the top line:

```
#include <SimpleDHT.h>
```

This is the command which says, "install the SimpleDHT library with the high-level commands in it." When you installed the library by going to the *Manage Library* option, you added this special set of code to the list of libraries the IDE could call.

Contained in this special code is the translation between the high-level commands we type in our sketch and the detailed commands the smart sensor understands.

In this sketch, there are really only two high level commands we need to pay attention to. The first is:

```
SimpleDHT11 dht11(pinDHT11);
```

It is very obtuse and hard to see what this command does. Basically, the first word, SimpleDHT11 is the command in the library to create an object which can perform a few actions and is connected to the specific pin number inside the ().

It is like we are creating a little robot which can do a limited number of pre-defined activities, like moving forward, or backward, or turning left or turning right, or picking up a block or reading a number written on the wall.

We call these little robots that can perform actions, *objects*. This is where the term, *Object Oriented Programming* (OOP) comes from.

The *object* this command creates is a thing, a *noun*. The noun can perform some actions which are verbs.

This command, SimpleDHT11, (remember, it is case sensitive) creates an object which we named *dht11*. We could have named this object

Harry or robotKiller, or sensor1. We have the flexibility of creating any name, as long as it has no funny characters in it.

Using the name *dht11* at least tells us what the object relates to. It names a thing that represents the DHT11 sensor.

To have our little robot perform an action, we append a verb to the end of its name, after a period. This format should look familiar. We use it in Serial.begin(). The object is Serial. This is the robot that is the name of the serial com link between the Arduino board and the USB port of the computer.

The action verb, begin, tells the Serial object to initialize communication at a specific baud rate, inside the ().

The action verb, .print() tells the Serial object, "send the characters inside the () over the com port."

The object *dht11* has only one action verb we will use in this sketch. It's rather obtusely hidden in the if statement, but here it is:

```
dht11.read(&temperature, &humidity, NULL))
```

The action verb is to .read the internal settings of the DHT11 sensor, which is connected on the digital pin with the variable name *pinDHT11*. The first term that is sent to the dht11 object is the pin value to which the sensor is connected. The .read command will read and return three variable values: the *temperature*, the *humidity* and another term which we don't care about.

Inside the library, the variables *temperature* and *humidity* are defined. These are special terms. The "and sign", &, in front of the terms, turns these terms into *pointers*. This means that somewhere in memory are the locations of the *temperature* and *humidity* variables.

The dht11.read() command will point to the location where the temperature and humidity numbers are stored and return in the variable names *temperature* and *humidity*, these values.

This is a very convoluted way of just grabbing the temperature and humidity measurements. But we have to do this, based on how the library was written.

And this library is one of the easier ones for the DHT11 sensor.

The DHT11 sensor cannot respond with a measurement faster than every 1.2 second. This means we have to add at least 1.2 second delay after taking a measurement before we can ask for another measurement. This is why there is a delay of 1.5 seconds.

While the code in this example works, it is way overkill for what we need. We can dramatically simplify it so that we can use the results of the temperature and humidity measurements in other projects.

We strip off all the non-essential code and just use the minimum to set up the sensor and read these two data points.

The complete, minimum sketch is:

```
#include <SimpleDHT.h>
SimpleDHT11 dht11;
byte temperature;
byte humidity;
int pinDHT11 = 4;

void setup() {
  Serial.begin(2000000);
}

void loop() {
  dht11.read(pinDHT11, &temperature, &humidity, NULL);
  Serial.print(temperature); Serial.print(" degC, ");
  Serial.print(humidity); Serial.println(" rH");
  delay(1500);
}
```

This is all the code we need to read temperature and humidity values from the smart sensor. We can use the terms temperature and humidity as variables. Stored in these variables are the latest values of the temperature and humidity.

Remember, this code will only run if you have already installed the **`<SimpleDHT.h>`** *library.*

When we run this sketch, we will print the current temperature and humidity. Figure 7.6 shows an example of the serial monitor showing the measured temperature and humidity.

```
COM5

23 degC, 29 rH
23 degC, 29 rH
23 degC, 29 rH
23 degC, 29 rH
23 degC, 30 rH
23 degC, 36 rH
23 degC, 40 rH
23 degC, 43 rH
23 degC, 46 rH
23 degC, 49 rH
24 degC, 51 rH
24 degC, 48 rH
24 degC, 45 rH
24 degC, 43 rH
24 degC, 41 rH
24 degC, 39 rH
24 degC, 38 rH
24 degC, 37 rH
24 degC, 36 rH
```

Figure 7.6 The measured temperature and humidity recorded in my house.

7.3 Sketch: Plotting the temperature and humidity

Now that we have a way of measuring these two environmental parameters and we can display them every 1 ½ seconds, we can plot either one on the serial plotter.

We need to select which term to plot and then print out each data point on a separate line.

Try this experiment: Modify the last sketch to plot the humidity and then the temperature. Select which one by commenting out the other.

Here is my sketch:

```
#include <SimpleDHT.h>
```

```
SimpleDHT11 dht11;
byte temperature;
byte humidity;
int pinDHT11 = 4;

void setup() {
  Serial.begin(2000000);
}

void loop() {
  dht11.read(pinDHT11, &temperature, &humidity, NULL);
  //Serial.println(temperature);
  Serial.println(humidity);
  delay(1500);
}
```

When I plotted the humidity, I placed my finger over the sensor for a few minutes and then moved it away. This recorded a spike in the humidity.

The time base corresponds to 100 points per division, at 1.5 sec/point, or a total time of 150 seconds per division, which is 2.5 minutes per division. Figure 7.7 shows the plotted humidity after I held my finger over the sensor.

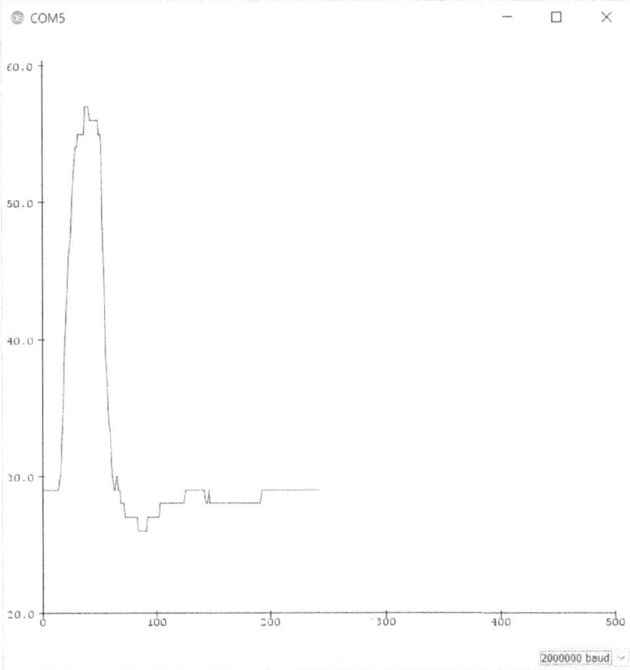

Figure 7.7. The humidity plotted with a time base of 2.5 min per division. The vertical scale is the humidity. I held my finger over the sensor for 1 minute and then removed it.

7.4 Datalogging data directly into a text file using a terminal emulator

So far, we looked at three ways of getting data from the Arduino:

- *printing directly on the Serial Monitor*
- *plotting directly on the Serial Plotter*
- *copying data from the Serial Monitor and pasting it into a spreadsheet*

In each case, the data was sent over the serial com link to the computer. The Arduino IDE has a built-in function which reads the data on the serial com link and does something with it.

The built in Serial Monitor is an example of a general tool called a *terminal emulator*. This is named for the "dumb" terminals consisting of a cathode ray tube (CRT) monitor and keyboard we used to use to communicate with computers in the "olden days."

When we emulate a simple terminal which just reads and writes data to and from the serial com link, we call it a *terminal* or *terminal emulator*.

The Serial Monitor is a very simple version of a terminal emulator. Once you set its baud rate to receive data to the same rate at which the Arduino is set to transmit using the Serial.begin() command, the Serial Monitor displays the characters transmitted on the serial com link.

It has a buffer to store the data as it comes in so we can scroll up and down the transmitted data.

As in most tools, there is a balance between feature richness and ease of use. In the case of the Serial Monitor, it is really easy to use, but doesn't really have many features.

However, there are other terminal emulator programs for any operating system which have more features.

Sparkfun offers a great review of terminal program options for all operating systems.

Of all the terminal emulators for windows, my favorite is *Yet Another Terminal* (YAT). You can Download it from this wiki page.

You will need to scroll to the bottom of this page and click on the large green "*download*" button. Once the .exe downloads, click on the .exe program to install it. Use all the default conditions.

Run the YAT program. When the program opens, you will see a simple screen, as shown in Figure 7.8. Before we can use it to read the data coming down the serial port, we have to adjust a few settings.

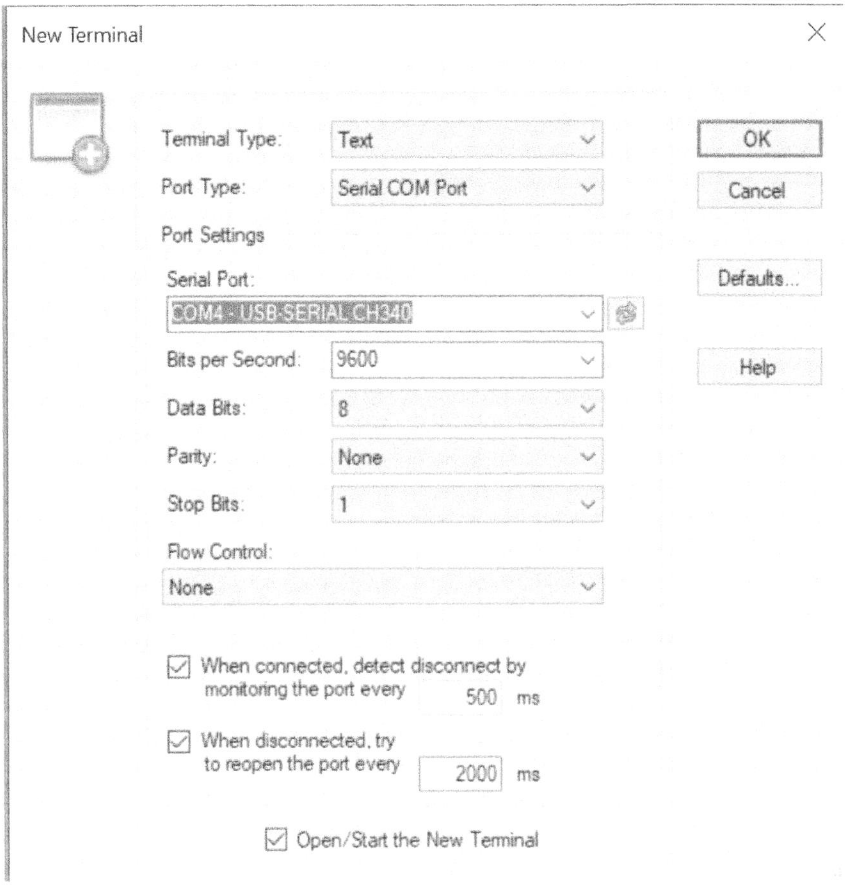

Figure 7.8 The opening screen for YAT.

If this page does not open, under the Terminal menu, scroll to the bottom and select the settings option, as shown in Figure 7.9.

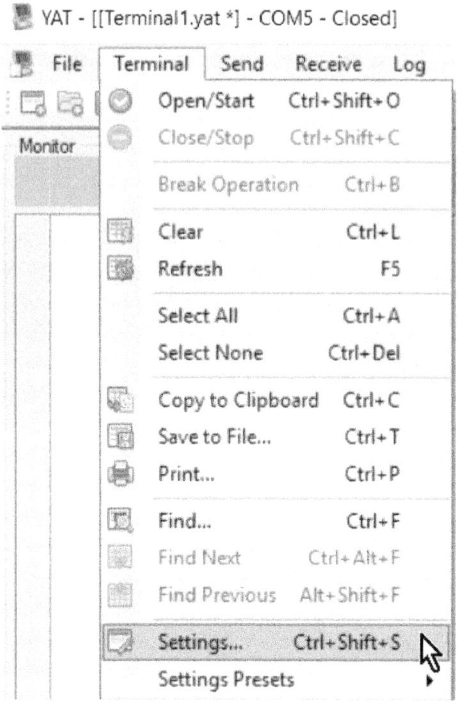

Figure 7.9 Select the Settings option in the Terminal menu.

When this screen opens up there are really only a few settings to adjust. The settings window is shown in Figure 7.10. Make sure your settings are set to these default values.

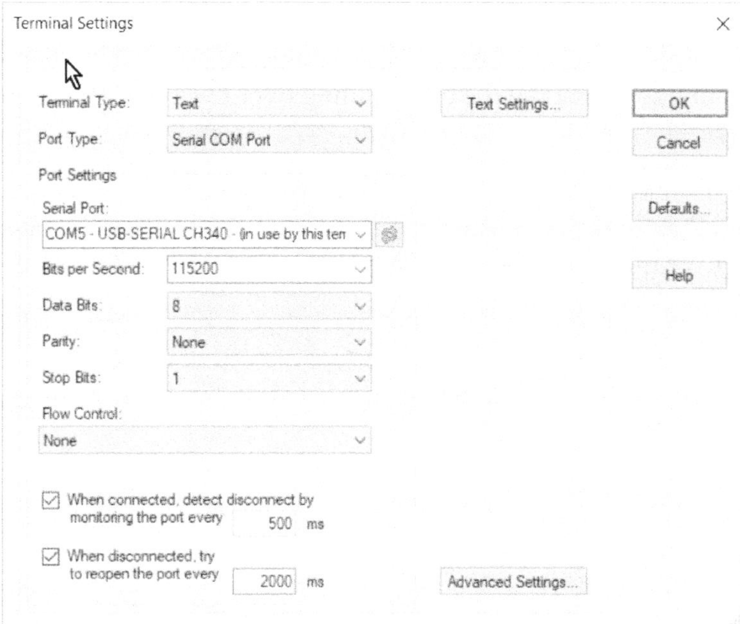

Figure 7.10. Select the com port and the baud rate to match the Arduino.

The two most important settings are the port connections and the baud rate. Take a look at the baud rate options. There is no 2,000,000 option.

These are the same two settings we had to adjust before we could use the Serial Monitor tool.

You can experiment with the highest baud rate you can send and receive reliable data just as we did in Arduinos Without Tears.

I found 115200 baud as the fastest, available speed that always worked.

Once these two settings are adjusted, the terminal is ready to read the serial monitor.

Only one device can be using the serial link at any time. To upload the sketch over the serial link, you first have to stop the terminal emulator. This is found under the Terminal menu. Select the start or stop command to stop the terminal monitor to upload the sketch, then turn on the monitor to display the data coming over the serial link from the Arduino.

We can use the most recent sketch in the previous section to print humidity data to the serial monitor. After we run this sketch, data is coming over the serial com link. We just need to turn YAT on to display this data.

Under the Terminal menu, select Start, as shown in Figure 7.11. When the terminal starts received data is displayed on the main window. This is where all the magic can happen.

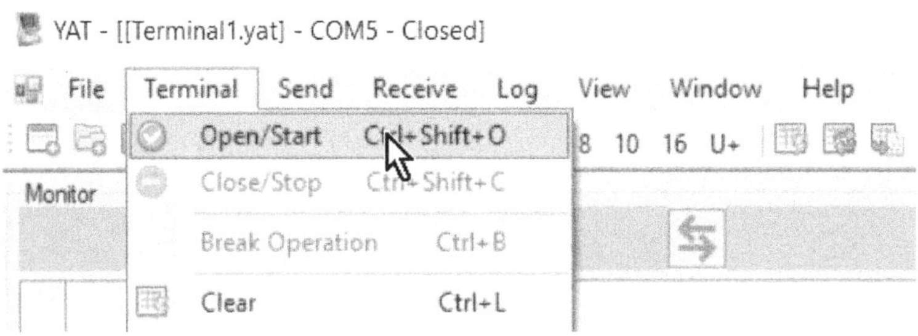

Figure 7.11. To have YAT display the data coming in over the serial monitor just click start, under the terminal menu.

In its simplest form, YAT will act just like the Serial Monitor. It will display the characters that come in over the serial com link, like as shown in Figure 7.12.

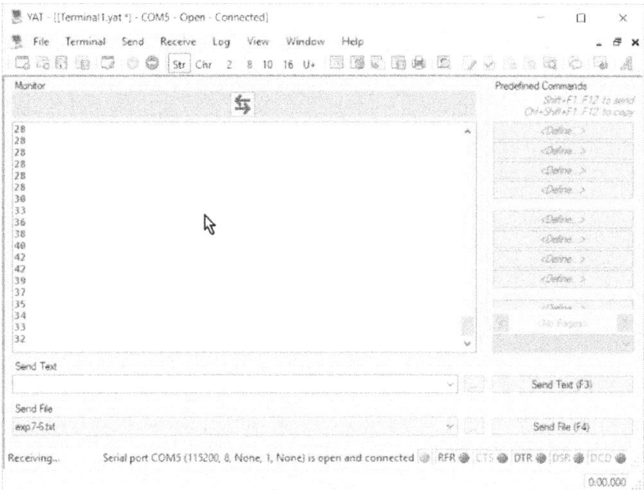

Figure 7.12 An example of the data read on YAT as it comes in from the Arduino just like on the Serial Monitor.

7.5 Experiment: data logging measurements with a date stamp

In addition to the data coming in from the Arduino, we can also add a date stamp, a time stamp and a delta time since the terminal opened, stamp. All of this information is added to the data by the computer. There are no changes we require the Arduino do to.

To activate these features, we pull down the View menu and select *Show Time Stamp* and *Show Time Span*, as shown in Figure 7.13.

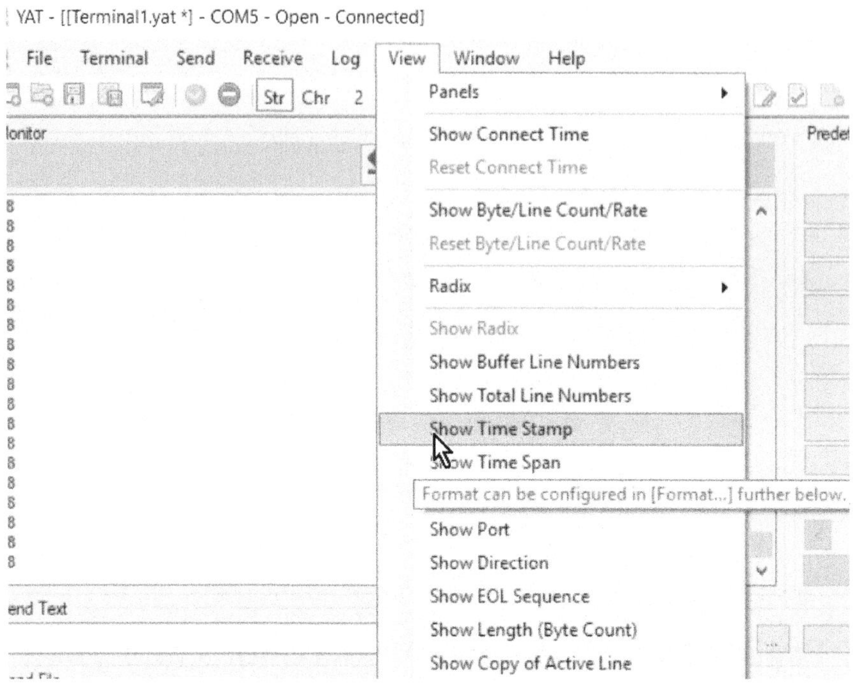

Figure 7.13. Under the View menu, select the Show time Stamp and Show Time Delta.

In addition, we can format the display of this information under the format item at the bottom of the View menu. The format screen allows us to create a convenient style for the data in the window. My own personal preference uses three important features:

1. *Use a **different color** for each type of data. This makes it easy to tell what is what in each column.*
2. *Use a **comma AND space** to separate the data on the monitor. This will help when exporting the data into a file.*
3. ***No enclosure**. This will print just the numbers, without brackets {} or parentheses ().*

My selections are shown in Figure 7.14.

Figure 7.14 Set the format for displaying the time stamp, time range and delimiters.

Using these settings, we can display the measured data from the Arduino with the date and timc for cach point and the time span from the time the terminal window was opened up.

All this data is added to the data coming over from the Arduino, based on the real time clock in the PC recording the serial com link. The final screen is shown in Figure 7.15. This is the data we want to save and later import into a spreadsheet.

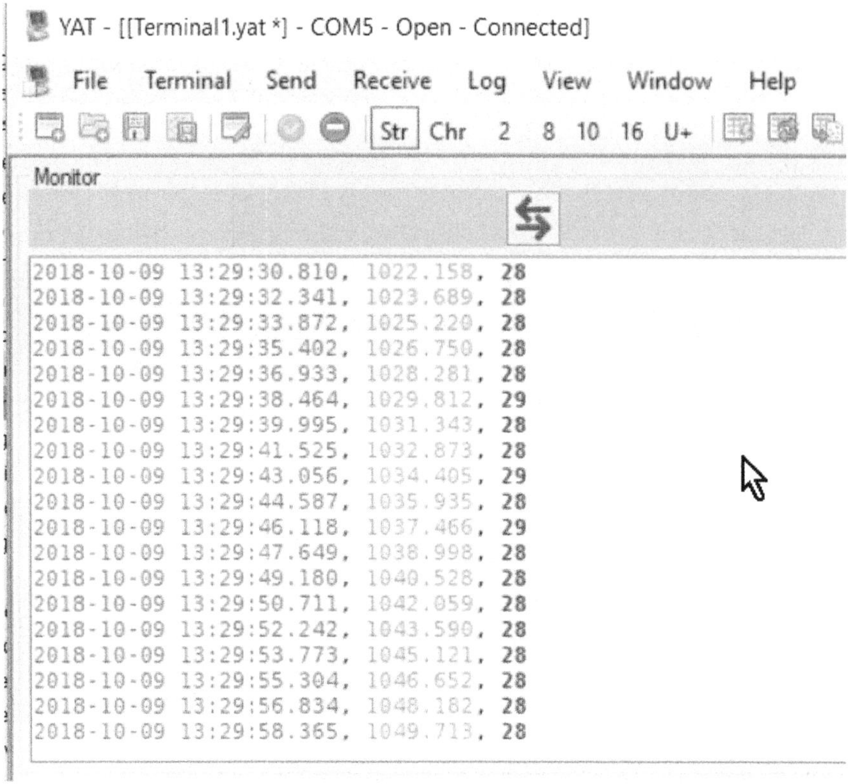

Figure 7.15 Final data recorded on the screen with the time stamp information and the Arduino data.

7.6 Experiment: Importing data from a text file directly into a spreadsheet

We've already seen how we can plot data directly as it comes from the Arduino using the Serial Plotter tool built into the Arduino IDE.

We've also seen that we can literally copy the data from the Serial Monitor and paste it into any spreadsheet. We can do the same from the YAT screen.

In addition, there is another way of getting data directly into a spreadsheet: save it to a file.

One of the cool features of YAT is to log the data that comes in over the serial link along with the time stamp information, directly into a text file. This file can be opened by any spreadsheet tool.

We can set YAT up to write each line of data that comes in on the serial com link into a file and save it as it comes in. This can be a text file and replicate exactly what you see on the screen.

This way we can save long records of data and not lose any of it and have it available for immediate import.

To set up YAT to data log the file, we open up the log menu item and select settings at the bottom of the list. This is shown in Figure 7.16.

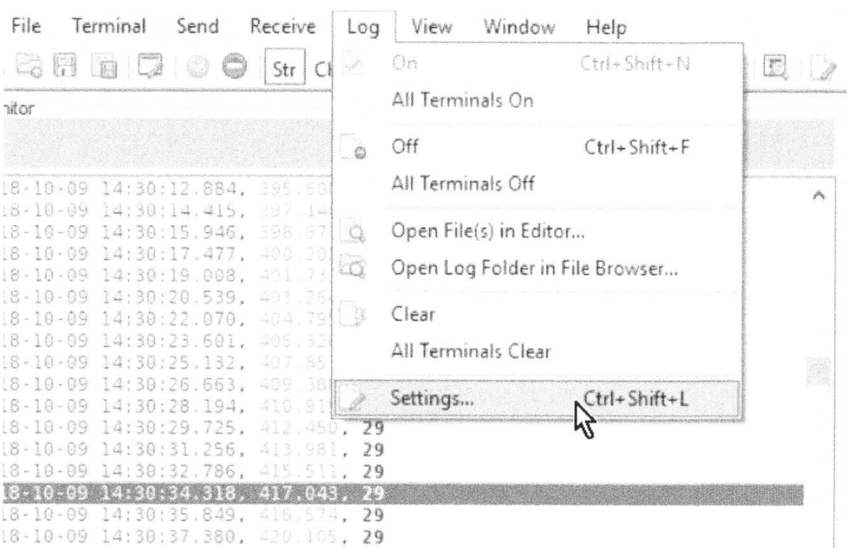

Figure 7.16 To set up a file for data logging, pull down the Log menu item and select the settings item at the bottom.

In this settings window, the most important settings, as shown in Figure 7.17 are:

- *The directory to store the log file.*
- *Use Neat outputs so that all the time stamp information is included*
- *Log received data*
- *If you select Append if file exists, every time you close the terminal and open it, the data will be written to the same file. I usually use this feature.*
- *If you select the Create separate files button, every time you stop the terminal and start it up, a new file will be created.*

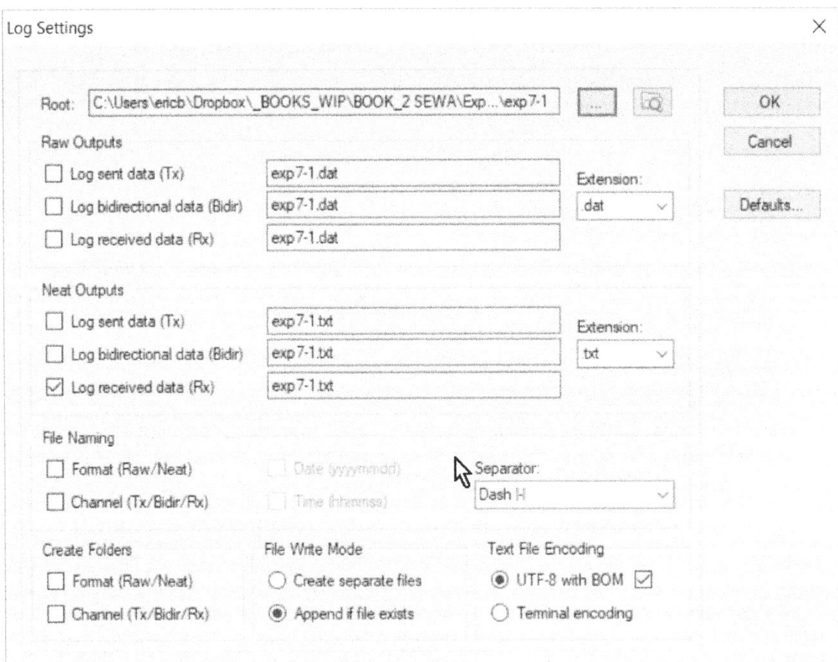

Figure 7.17 We want to find a directly to place the log file and use the settings as marked.

Once the log setup is complete, it's a simple matter of selecting log on from the log menu and instantly, you are creating a file with the serial data and its date stamp information.

Figure 7.18 is an example of the data in the text file. The first column is the date, then the time and then the elapsed time since the terminal window was opened and finally, the humidity data.

```
exp7-12.txt - Notepad
File  Edit  Format  View  Help
2018-10-09 14:53:39.810, 013.727, 29
2018-10-09 14:53:41.340, 015.257, 29
2018-10-09 14:53:42.871, 016.788, 29
2018-10-09 14:53:44.403, 018.320, 29
2018-10-09 14:53:45.934, 019.851, 29
2018-10-09 14:53:47.465, 021.382, 29
2018-10-09 14:53:48.995, 022.912, 29
2018-10-09 14:53:50.525, 024.442, 29
2018-10-09 14:53:52.057, 025.974, 29
2018-10-09 14:53:53.588, 027.505, 29
2018-10-09 14:53:55.118, 029.035, 29
2018-10-09 14:53:56.650, 030.567, 29
2018-10-09 14:53:58.181, 032.098, 29
2018-10-09 14:53:59.712, 033.629, 29
2018-10-09 14:54:01.242, 035.159, 29
2018-10-09 14:54:02.773, 036.690, 29
2018-10-09 14:54:04.304, 038.221, 29
2018-10-09 14:54:05.835, 039.752, 29
2018-10-09 14:54:07.365, 041.282, 29
```

Figure 7.18. An example of the data stored in the text file using the YAT logging feature.

This data is automatically saved and ready for import into a spreadsheet.

We can open this text file with a spreadsheet tool, like Excel and separate each column of data into a separate column in the spreadsheet. The only secret is to use the delimit option to convert the text file into columns of meaningful data. An example of doing this is shown in Figure 7.19.

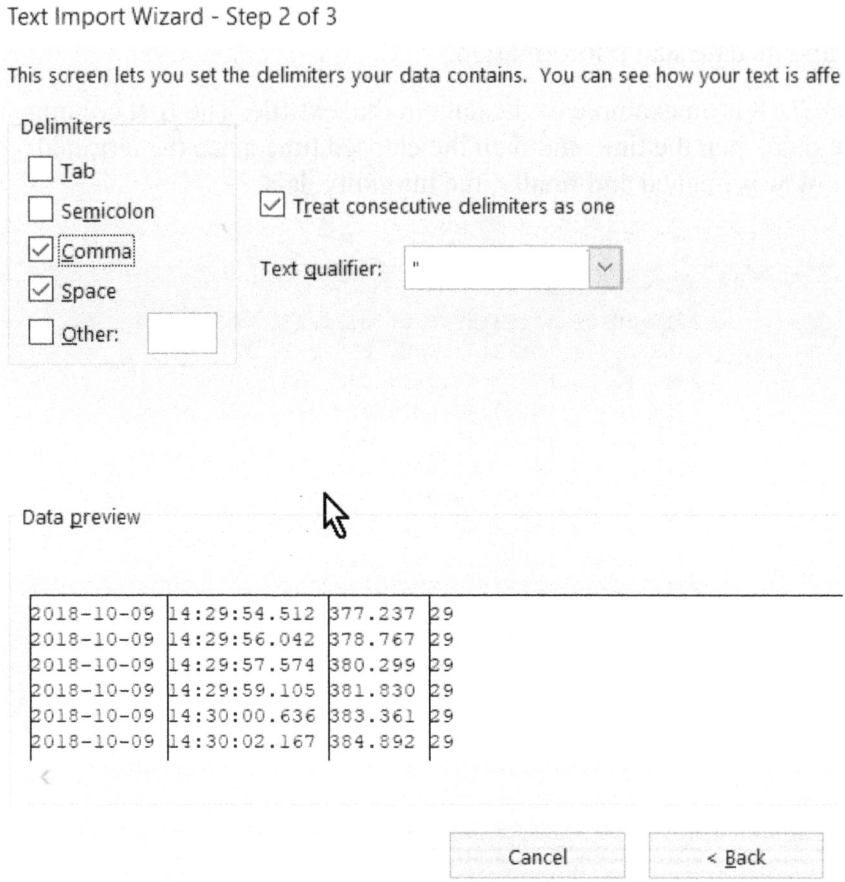

Figure 7.19. When opening a txt file in excel you are given the option how to interpret the columns. Select delimit and comma and space for perfect importing.

Once in excel, we can turn on the power of spreadsheet analysis and plotting.

7.7 New technique: averaging over some number of samples

So far in this chapter, we have unleashed the power to:

- *import the library for a smart sensor*
- *modify an example sketch for what we want to do*
- *send temperature and humidity data from a smart sensor to the serial monitor*
- *display or plot the measured temperature or humidity data*
- *open up terminal window and data log the measurements with a time stamp*
- *automatically log the measurements and their time stamp in a file*
- *open the saved data in a spreadsheet to analyze and plot the data*

There is one last step we would like to accomplish. The fastest we can take a measurement is about once every 1.5 seconds. This is limited by how quickly the analog front end and digital interface can refresh a measurement.

But, the response time of the sensor is slower than this rate, so there is no point in trying to take data any faster.

In fact, since the environment will change very slowly, we can take data slower, and save the measurements over a longer period of time.

The resolution of the sensor output is not very high. We can only get about 1 degC and 1% rh as the resolution. There will not be much advantage in averaging in this case, but it might help a little bit. At the very least, it will mean we collect the data for a longer period of time and have fewer data points, making it a little more manageable.

In its simplest form, all we have to do is average n consecutive data points. Since we are logging the time we printed the data, we know what time the averaged value was taken.

Try this experiment. How would you modify the code to average n number of readings for both the temperature and humidity and print them out and write them to a file?

After you give it a try, take a look at my code.

7.8 Sketch: Record and data log DHT11 data to the serial monitor

```
#include <SimpleDHT.h>
SimpleDHT11 dht11;
byte temperature;
byte humidity;
float TimeAve_sec = 10.0;
int iDelay_msec = 1500;
int pinDHT11 = 4;
int nptsAve = TimeAve_sec * 1000 / iDelay_msec;
float tempAve_degC;
float humidAve_rh;

void setup() {
  Serial.begin(115200);
  pinMode(13, OUTPUT);
  pinMode(12, OUTPUT);
}

void loop() {
  tempAve_degC = 0.0;
  humidAve_rh = 0.0;
  for (int i = 1; i <= nptsAve; i++) {
    digitalWrite(13, HIGH);
    dht11.read(pinDHT11, &temperature, &humidity, NULL);
    digitalWrite(13, LOW);
    tempAve_degC = tempAve_degC + temperature;
    humidAve_rh = humidAve_rh + humidity;
    delay(iDelay_msec);
  }
```

```
    digitalWrite(12, HIGH);
    tempAve_degC = tempAve_degC / nptsAve;
    humidAve_rh = humidAve_rh / nptsAve;

    Serial.print(tempAve_degC); Serial.print(", ");
    Serial.println(humidAve_rh);
    digitalWrite(12, LOW);
}
```

I added two other slight modifications. I like getting some sort of feedback when the sketch is working. I added the blue LED to flash when it sampled the smart sensor, so I know it is asking for a new reading. Then I added the red LED to flash when it is writing the data to the serial monitor.

This way I have a little feedback that the Arduino is taking data on schedule.

7.9 New technique: averaging over some period of time

The second way we can average real time measurements is by a period of time, rather than just a fixed number of samples.

We'll still keep track of the running average, but will also have to keep track of the number of samples we are adding up. When we reach the total time we want to average over, we will stop the collecting and calculate the average value.

Instead of a for loop, we'll use a while loop. The format is

While (this statement is true){

Execute this code

}

We stay inside the while loop collecting the data and the averaging until the timer gets above the value we were waiting for.

We need to introduce a few new variables to keep track of the time and the number of samples we are measuring.

Try this experiment: How would you modify the sketch above to average for a fixed amount of time, rather than a fixed number of measurement? When you have given it a try, take a look at my sketch. Remember, there are often times multiple right answers.

7.10 Sketch: averaging over a period of time

```
#include <SimpleDHT.h>
SimpleDHT11 dht11;
byte temperature;
byte humidity;
float TimeAve_sec = 10.0;
int iDelay_msec = 1500;
int pinDHT11 = 4;
int nptsAve = TimeAve_sec * 1000 / iDelay_msec;
float tempAve_degC;
float humidAve_rh;
long nCounts_measured;

void setup() {
  Serial.begin(115200);
  pinMode(13, OUTPUT);
  pinMode(12, OUTPUT);
}

void loop() {
  tempAve_degC = 0.0;
  humidAve_rh = 0.0;
  for (int i = 1; i <= nptsAve; i++) {
    digitalWrite(13, HIGH);
    dht11.read(pinDHT11, &temperature, &humidity, NULL);
    digitalWrite(13, LOW);
    tempAve_degC = tempAve_degC + temperature;
    humidAve_rh = humidAve_rh + humidity;
    delay(iDelay_msec);
  }
  digitalWrite(12, HIGH);
  tempAve_degC = tempAve_degC / nptsAve;
  humidAve_rh = humidAve_rh / nptsAve;
```

```
  Serial.print(tempAve_degC); Serial.print(", ");
  Serial.println(humidAve_rh);
  digitalWrite(12, LOW);
}
```

7.11 Experiment: monitoring the environment- inside and outside

In this chapter, we've developed a great tool to measure the environmental parameters of temperature and humidity. As a measure of personal comfort, a resolution of 1 degC and 1% rh is just fine. Our sensations can't resolve even this coarse a resolution. I used an averaging time of about 10 seconds, just to consolidate some of the data.

With this tool, I measured the ambient environment in my house for a short period of time, and then took my laptop, Arduino and multi-function board outside, while it was cold and rainy and recorded another hour of temperature and humidity. Then I brought it inside.

All the while, I data logged the measurements into a text file. Altogether, I had data for 7,000 seconds of elapsed time, which is about 2 hours.

I opened this file with excel and plotted the temperature and humidity against the elapsed time. This data was imported into excel and plotted. The graph of the measured results over the two-hour period is shown in Figure 7.20.

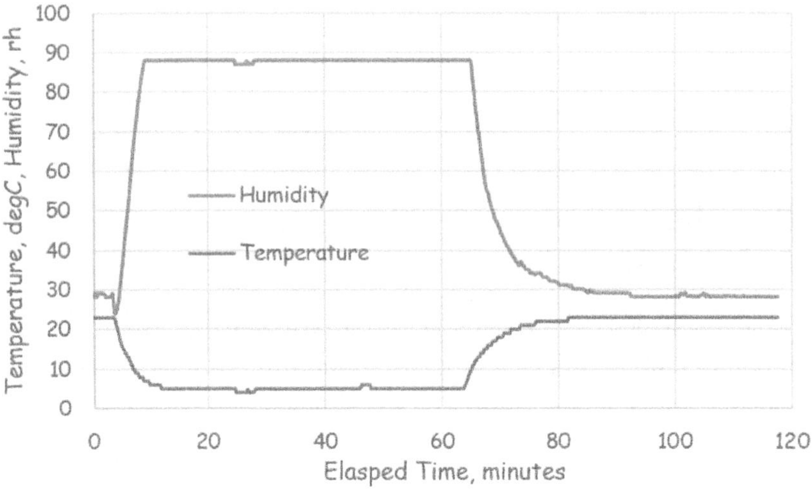

Figure 7.20. Plotted temperature and humidity over a two-hour period. The measurements include some time inside the house and outside while it was cold and wet.

Try this experiment: How does the ambient temperature and humidity vary in your home? If you use a 1-minute averaging time, you can record a day's worth of measurements in 1400 readings.

7.12 Summary of the commands introduced so far

Command	Description

void setup (){
 	
}
	This is a function that appears in EVERY sketch. Every command within the brackets will be executed just once

void loop (){
 	
}
	This is a function that appears in EVERY sketch. Every command within the brackets will execute over and over again.

pinMode(13, OUTPUT);	This command tells the Arduino that we are going to use a specific digital pin as an OUTPUT, as distinct from an INPUT. We use the pin number to identify the pin we want to setup.
digitalWrite(13, HIGH);	This command controls the output of a digital pin and makes it either a HIGH (logic 1, or 5 V) or a LOW (a logic 0 or a 0 V). Once executed, the pin value will be set to this value.
delay(1000);	This command for tell the Arduino to sit there, twiddling its thumbs, doing nothing for a duration of milliseconds as listed inside the (). In this example, the time interval to wait is 1000 msec = 1 sec.
// or /* */	Everything after these two forward slashes will be ignored by the Arduino sketch. We can use this add comments for our own benefit on any line. For multiple lines add them between the /* and the */ lines.
delayMicroseconds(1000);	Just like the delay() function, this function will force the Arduino to sit there and do nothing, for a time duration equal to the time, in microseconds inside the (). In this examples, 1000 microseconds = 1 msec = 0.001 sec.
Serial.begin(9600);	This command opens up the serial com link with a baud rated inside the (). In this example the baud rate is 9600 baud. The name Serial is an object, the serial link. The .begin is a verb, telling the object to get set up.

`Serial.print("Hello World");`	This command will print characters to the serial communications channel. Everything inside the () will be printed. To print a string, enclose the characters within quotes. After printing, the cursor will be left on the same line.
`Serial.println(" ");`	Does the same thing as the `Serial.print` command, but moves the cursor to the next line after printing the characters.
`int`	We use this to assign a variable name as a new variable. It is place at the beginning of the sketch. We have to assign a variable name to a type of variable. This command creates a variable that is a + or – whole number up to 2^{15} = 32, 767
`long`	This assigns a variable name to a + and – whole number up to 2^31 = 2,147, 483, 647. Use this when we expect to be counting very large number. You can never go wrong making all integer variables Long variable.
`float`	This assigns a variable as a floating-point number, which is any number having a decimal point. Use this command when the variable needs to have a decimal point.

`for (int i = 1; i <= 10; i++) {`
`  //execute this code if i<=10`
`}`
	This is a loop that causes all the code within the { and } brackets to execute for a certain number of times. Inside the () of the command are three sections, separated by ;. The first sets up the index that will step, and its initial value. The second, sets up the condition. While this is true the loop continues. When it is false, the loop breaks to after the }. The last section increments the index, i, by 1.

`sin(Phase_rad)`	This function returns the value of the sine of the number inside the (), assuming this number is an angle in radians. 2 x π radians = 360 deg.
digitalRead(5)	This command will read the digital value of the pin number inside the (), 5, in this example, and return the value as a 0 or 1 or false or true. Once executed, this command becomes the value it reads.
millis()	This function returns the value of the internal counter which is counting the number of milliseconds since the beginning of the sketch. Nothing is placed inside the (). This is a long integer. Every time it is called, it becomes the current value of milliseconds.
micros()	This function returns the value of the internal timer, which is counting up microseconds since the start of the sketch. The resolution is 4 microseconds. Nothing is placed inside the (). This is a long integer. Every time it is called, it becomes the current value of microseconds.

`while (i>1) {` `}`	This command will cause all the code within the {…} to execute over and over again, as long as the condition inside the (…) is true.
`random(min, max);`	This command returns a random integer value that is between the min value and the (max-1) value. The random number returned is a long integer.
`#include <SimpleDHT.h>`	The include command tells the Arduino to go to the list of libraries you have installed using the library manager and grab the one identified in the <…>. Then add all the commands listed in this library to the commands available for this sketch. It's like we are adding some new vocabulary words to what the Arduino understands.
`SimpleDHT11 dht11(pinDHT11);`	The command, `SimpleDHT11` is a specific command in the library we included in the previous statement. It tells the Arduino to create a new object, called dht11. The number in the () is the value of the digital pin that is connected to the DHT11 sensor. Once this object is created, we can make it do things by appending verbs to its end separated by a period.

Chapter 8. Data Logging Directly into an Excel Spreadsheet

In the last experiment, we recorded the time and date stamp and the temperature and humidity data and wrote all this data into a text file using a free terminal emulation software tool. We could then open the file using any spreadsheet and use the plotting features of a spreadsheet to plot the data.

If you have a PC and run Microsoft Excel, you can record the information that comes over the serial port directly, write it into the columns of an excel spreadsheet and plot the data as comes in.

To accomplish this, we will use a free software tool called PLX-DAX v2.

8.1 New Tool: PLX-DAQ v2

In this section, I will introduce you to PLX-DAQ v2, which is a simple to use macro written inside MS excel to automatically read the serial port and move the readings directly into the spreadsheet.

The original version of PLX-DAQ was written for the PIC microcontroller. It worked in some cases for the Arduino but was limited in functionality.

This tool was re-written from scratch and dramatically improved by Jonathan Arndt, who goes by the handle Net^Devil.

The latest version of this tool can be downloaded from here. As of this writing, the latest version is version v2.11. Always download the latest version.

The software is basically an excel spreadsheet with an embedded macro. Unfortunately, it only runs on a windows version of excel since it heavily uses the macros built into excel.

All it really does is read (or write) data on the serial com port, sent over to it from your Arduino sketch. The macro reads this data and carries out the commands based on key words it reads. Simple commands are built into the macro.

On the Arduino, we just print a few keywords to the com port, which are read and understood by this macro. The macro in excel reads the serial port and follows the commands it receives.

To write data directly into the excel spreadsheet, we run the code in the sketch. Then we open up an excel file that has this macro running.

This free software tool will enable us to take information from the Arduino, like measured data, write it into an excel spreadsheet, plot it as we go, and save the worksheet, all automatically.

The way we do this is by adding the directions to excel as code words in an Arduino sketch. When these code words are printed to the serial com port and read by the macro running inside excel, the macro will direct excel to do things for us automatically like printing labels to columns, printing data into specific columns and even saving the worksheet.

In this first simple experiment, we will take advantage of just five key-word commands we will embed in an Arduino sketch:

CLEARSHEET: when this keyword is printed on the serial com link by the Arduino code, the excel macro will read it and clear all the data on the active worksheet, including the labels. If you are starting a new experiment and want to initialize the spreadsheet for new data, this should be the first command sent over the serial link.

The command in the Arduino sketch would be

Serial.println("CLEARSHEET");

CLEARDATA: this command, when received by the excel macro from the serial link, will clear only the data in the spreadsheet starting at row 2 and moving down the spreadsheet. It will retain the labels which are printed in row 1.

The command in the Arduino sketch would be:

Serial.println("CLEARDATA");

LABEL: this command will write the titles for the columns in the excel spreadsheet. Its format is

Serial.println("LABEL, 1st column, 2nd column, 3rd column, last column");

DATA: this is the fundamental command to write some information into the next row of the spreadsheet. The information after the DATA command will be parsed into the next row with each set of data separated by a comma, parsed into each column.

The command in the Arduino sketch to print two variables into two different columns would be:

```
Serial.println("DATA,");
Serial.print(var1);Serial.print(", ");
Serial.println(var2);
```

SAVEWORKBOOK: when this keyword is sent to the serial port, the macro will save the current worksheet using the file name it had when you opened it.

These key words are added to a sketch and placed in Serial.print statements so they are printed to the serial com.

The excel spreadsheet will listen to the com port and read these key words. The macro will perform internal operations based on the key words it reads.

In the spreadsheet, we will insert an excel graph so we can not only save the data to the excel file, but also plot it as it comes in.

8.2 Recording and plotting data

In this first example, we will only set up excel to record some dummy data and plot it as we go.

The most common application for PLX-DAQ is to data log data at specific time intervals. In this sort of application, the exact date and time each data point was recorded might be important. In this case, we can take advantage of three built in key words used by the macro to track time.

In addition to writing variables into each cell in the excel spreadsheet, we can use special key words which the macro will translate into specific values or actions.

There are three specific key words we will use to tell the macro to print time information. They are:

The keyword ***DATE*** is read by the macro and printed in the cell as the current date.

The keyword ***TIME*** is read by the macro and printed in the cell as the current time.

The keyword ***TIMER*** is read by the macro and printed in the cell as seconds since the start of pressing the connect button.

In this example, we will set up five columns in excel. They will be:

- *Current date (we will use the **DATE** key word)*
- *Current time (we will use the **TIME** key word)*
- *Elapsed time in seconds (we will use the **TIMER** key word)*
- *The number of points we have exported*
- *A random number from 0 to 9*

The first step is to clear out the spreadsheet and start from scratch. The CLEARSHEET command will erase all the columns but WILL NOT erase the plots we have on the spreadsheet, just the data.

This way, if we have a plot template we like, we just keep it and can still clear the spreadsheet.

The second step is to print the labels of each column in the first row.

The last step is to start printing the data into each column.

The code to clear the sheet and write the labels will only happen once, so should be placed in the void setup() function. It would look like this:

```
void setup() {
  Serial.begin(2000000);
  Serial.println("CLEARSHEET"); // clears sheet
  Serial.println("LABEL, Date, Time, Timer, Count,
Random");
}
```

Notice that we are sending data over the serial port at 2000000 baud. We can use any data rate the channel is capable of as long as we use the same value in the macro.

When the excel spreadsheet opens up, we will see the control panel for the macros, as displayed in Figure 8.1.

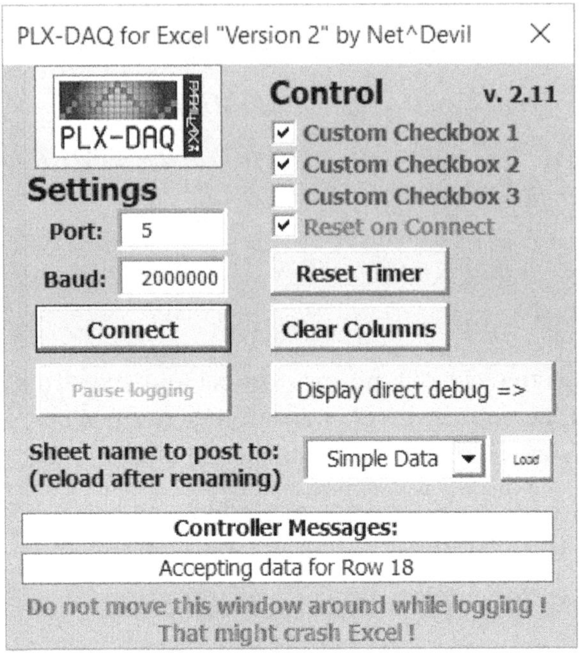

Figure 8.1. The control panel for the macro, displayed in the open excel workbook. Note that the baud rate and com port must match the same as the baud rate set up in the sketch and the com port for the Arduino.

The complete sketch to calculate the random number and print out the data is the following:

```
// simple test of the PLX-DAQ
int i = 0;
void setup() {
  Serial.begin(2000000);
  Serial.println("CLEARSHEET"); // clears sheet
  Serial.println("LABEL, Date, Time, Timer, Count, Random");
}
void loop() {
  Serial.print("DATA, DATE, TIME, TIMER,");
  Serial.print(i++); Serial.print(",");
  Serial.println(random(0, 10));
  delay(200);
}
```

We need to add one line in the beginning of the sketch to declare the variable, i, as an integer. We use this to count the number of iterations.

The first line in the `void loop` () function will print the first three columns of information to the macros. The key word DATA in the beginning will be read by the macro as a command. It will consider all the following terms as information to be placed in the spreadsheet cells.

The following three keywords, DATE, TIME, TIMER will be read by the macro which will tell it to print the current date, time and time in seconds since the start of the connect, to be printed in the consecutive cells on the same row.

The next two lines will print specific numbers in the next cells on the same row. It's not until the last command, Serial.println() is received that the last data will be placed at the end of the row and then the line feed command in the `Serial.println`() line will start printing the data on the next row of the excel spreadsheet.

I added a delay(100); as the last line just so that the data will come into the excel spreadsheet slow enough for excel to read it. There are some limits to how fast we can print data into the macro. We will explore these limits in a follow-on experiment.

Once this sketch has been uploaded to the Arduino, it will start printing all the lines to the serial com link.

To actually have this data come into excel, we have to run the macro by pressing the "Connect" button in the PLX-DAQ control box.

When we press the Connect button, the macro will send a reset command to the Arduino. This will force the Arduino to start the sketch from the beginning. The spreadsheet will be cleared, the labels will be printed and data will start to appear.

An example of the spreadsheet with some data, is shown in Figure 8.2.

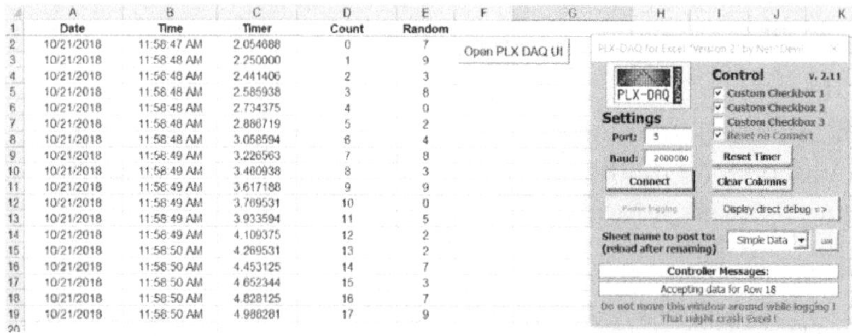

	A	B	C	D	E
1	Date	Time	Timer	Count	Random
2	10/21/2018	11:58:47 AM	2.054688	0	7
3	10/21/2018	11:58:48 AM	2.250000	1	9
4	10/21/2018	11:58:48 AM	2.441406	2	3
5	10/21/2018	11:58:48 AM	2.585938	3	8
6	10/21/2018	11:58:48 AM	2.734375	4	0
7	10/21/2018	11:58:48 AM	2.886719	5	2
8	10/21/2018	11:58:48 AM	3.058594	6	4
9	10/21/2018	11:58:49 AM	3.226563	7	8
10	10/21/2018	11:58:49 AM	3.400938	8	3
11	10/21/2018	11:58:49 AM	3.617188	9	9
12	10/21/2018	11:58:49 AM	3.789531	10	0
13	10/21/2018	11:58:49 AM	3.933594	11	5
14	10/21/2018	11:58:49 AM	4.109375	12	2
15	10/21/2018	11:58:50 AM	4.289531	13	2
16	10/21/2018	11:58:50 AM	4.453125	14	7
17	10/21/2018	11:58:50 AM	4.652344	15	3
18	10/21/2018	11:58:50 AM	4.828125	16	7
19	10/21/2018	11:58:50 AM	4.988281	17	9

Figure 8.2. An example of the data as displayed in excel for this simple sketch.

Since the data is now in an excel spreadsheet, we can take advantage of the power of excel and plot the data as it comes in.

With a little sample data already present, we select the columns we want to plot like D and E, and then insert a graph. For this example, I like an x-y scatter plot. We will plot the data in column D, the counter, as the x, horizontal axis, and the random values, in column E, as the Y or vertical values.

When the graph icon is inserted, the data already in columns D and E will be plotted. If the entire columns were selected, then both axes will be auto scaled by default. As new data comes in with higher count values, the graph will automatically adjust to fit and plot this new data.

Figure 8.3 shows an example with a simple plot inserted and data plotted as it comes in.

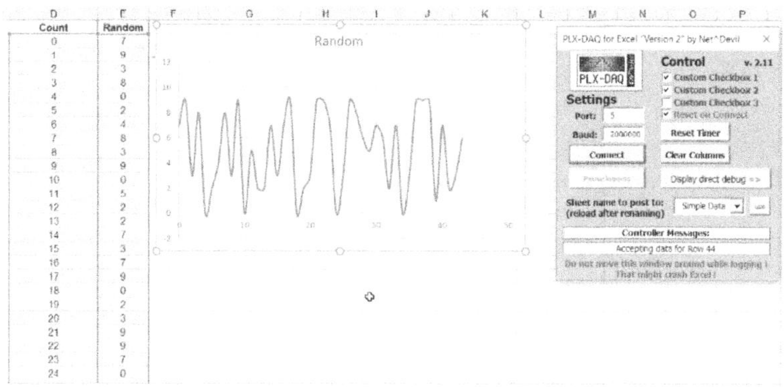

Figure 8.3. An example of the simple plot of the data in the excel spreadsheet as it comes in.

8.3 Two problems to avoid

There are two important problems to watch out for.

Problem #1: When the rate at which data comes into excel is faster than it can be plotted, you will lose some data and excel may crash.

Plotting each data point as it comes in takes some computing overhead by excel. This means when it is plotting the data, it is not listening to the serial port and getting the data to plot.

There is a small buffer in the com port. When data is read from the com buffer, it is removed from the com buffer and room is made for new data. When the rate at which the buffer is filled by writing from the Arduino sketch is faster than the rate at which the data is read and cleared by excel, the buffer can overload, and you lose some data.

In this simple sketch, we adjust the rate at which data is written to the serial port using the delay() function.

The fastest rate excel can read the data and plot it as it comes in is a little faster than 5 samples per second. This means the delay() function should be at least 200 msec to not overload the buffer, lose data and possibly crash excel.

A delay of 100 msec sends data over the com port too fast for excel to keep up. Pretty soon, we get a gap in the received data. This appears in the graph, as shown in Figure 8.4.

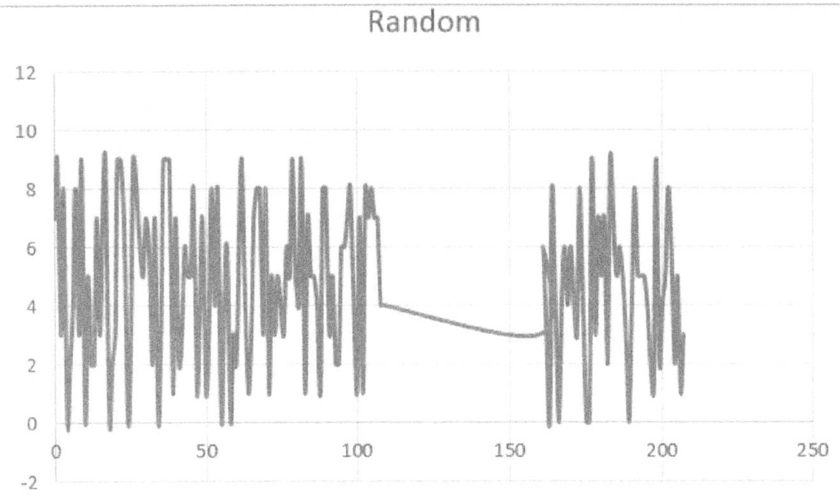

Figure 8.4. An example of printing data with a 100 msec delay showing a gap in receiving data when the plotting takes too much time and we are losing data.

To avoid this problem, we want to send data over the com port at a slow enough rate. A delay of 200 msec will allow the data to be plotted at the same rate at which it comes in.

Try this experiment: Starting with a delay of 200 msec, decrease the delay time and let at least 200 points come in. What is the shortest delay that will give stable readings?

Problem #2: In order to upload code to the Arduino when we load a new sketch, the com port cannot also be open by the excel macro.

This means to upload a new or modified sketch to the Arduino, we have to make sure the PLX-DAQ macro has been disconnected. The "connect" switch toggles back and forth between "connect" and "disconnect."

Luckily, this is a simple problem to avoid. If you get an error that upload to the Arduino failed, chances are, it is because the macro is still connected to the com port. Just press disconnect and try uploading to the Arduino again.

8.4 Sketch: Record temperature and humidity data into excel and plot it

All the pieces are together to data log data into excel and plot it as we go.

We start with the sketch we used before to log temperature and humidity data into a text file.

To this sketch, we add the lines to set up the spreadsheet, set the labels and print the data columns. The entire sketch is shown here:

```
#include <SimpleDHT.h>
SimpleDHT11 dht11;
byte temperature;
byte humidity;

float TimeAve_sec = 2;
int iDelay_msec = 1500;
int pinDHT11 = 4;

float TimeNow_hrs;
long iTimeStart_msec;

int nptsAve = TimeAve_sec * 1000 / iDelay_msec;
float tempAve_degC;
float humidAve_rh;

void setup() {

  pinMode(13, OUTPUT);
  pinMode(12, OUTPUT);
  Serial.begin(2000000);
  Serial.println("CLEARSHEET");
  Serial.println("LABEL,Date,Time,TimeNow(hrs),Temperature,Humidity");
  iTimeStart_msec = millis();
}

void loop() {
  tempAve_degC = 0.0;
  humidAve_rh = 0.0;
  for (int i = 1; i <= nptsAve; i++) {
    digitalWrite(13, HIGH);
    dht11.read(pinDHT11, &temperature, &humidity, NULL);
    digitalWrite(13, LOW);
    tempAve_degC = tempAve_degC + temperature;
```

```
    humidAve_rh = humidAve_rh + humidity;
    delay(iDelay_msec);
  }
  digitalWrite(12, HIGH);
  TimeNow_hrs = 0.001 * (millis() - iTimeStart_msec) / 3600.0;
  tempAve_degC = tempAve_degC / nptsAve;
  humidAve_rh = humidAve_rh / nptsAve;

  Serial.print("DATA, DATE"); Serial.print(", ");
  Serial.print("TIME"); Serial.print(", ");
  Serial.print(TimeNow_hrs, 3); Serial.print(", ");
  Serial.print(tempAve_degC); Serial.print(", ");
  Serial.println(humidAve_rh);
  digitalWrite(12, LOW);
}
```

This sketch will post the data to the serial port. The macro in excel will read the data and place incoming data into a new row in the spreadsheet.

The delay between posting new data is at least 1.5 sec, due to the inherent delay in reading the smart DHT11 sensor.

This means we have no problems plotting the data as we go. I inserted a simple xy scatter chart to plot both the temperature and humidity, on the same scale, as the data comes in. This is shown in Figure 8.5.

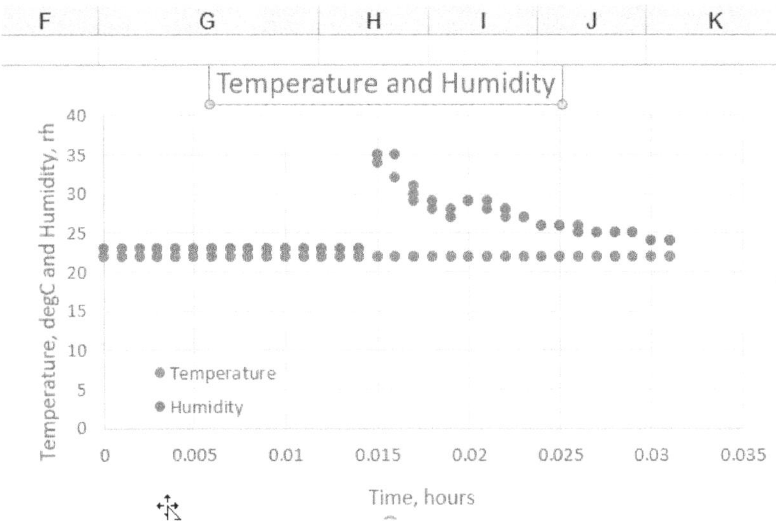

Figure 8.5. The spreadsheet showing some of the data inserted in excel, with the real time plot. Note the point where I breathed on the sensor.

As more data comes in, this plot will automatically scale the axes to include all the data.

To complete our data logger, we need to add the ability to periodically save the spreadsheet so that we don't lose much data if something happens to the computer.

8.5 Automatically saving a workbook

The key word to have the macro execute a save command for the current workbook is ***SAVEWORKBOOK***. We want to be sure to save the current workbook periodically so that we don't lose much data.

We should choose an interval that is long enough to not take up a lot of overhead but short enough so we don't lose too much data if the computer crashes.

Depending on the application, about every 10 minutes is a good saving interval.

We need to keep track of the current time when each data point is recorded and when the time reaches the time we want to save the workbook and we should execute a ***SAVEWORKBOOK*** command.

Try this experiment: How would you implement this routine?

The special command I added is an if statement. I created a new variable, iTimeLastSave_msec as the counter keeping track of when the last save happened. When the current time is after the save interval + last save time, we save again.

If the current time is greater than the time we should save again, we execute the save command. This is done in the following code:

```
if (millis() > (iTimeLastSave_msec + iSaveEvery_min * 60 * 1000)) {
    Serial.print(", ");  Serial.println("saved");
    Serial.println("SAVEWORKBOOK");
    iTimeLastSave_msec = millis();
  }
```

```
  else {
    Serial.println("");
  }
```

When implementing this algorithm, there is one very important potential problem to pay attention to.

There are two ways of storing integer information, as an int and as a long. They differ by up to how high a whole number they can count. An int can count up to 32,768, while a long can count up to over 2,147,483,648.

When we create an integer as an int, all the arithmetic we do with the number will be calculated as int math. If in the calculation, the result is over 32,768, it will roll over and may appear as a negative number.

If we want to do any future calculations using integer math, which might result in a number greater than 32,768, we should be sure to declare all the integer variables as long. This will keep all the digits we need through all the calculation.

This is especially important for the iSaveEvery_min variable. While this number will only be as much as 100, easily stored as an int, it is used in calculations which could result in numbers as high as 100,000. If we created this variable as an int, it would roll over when it is larger than 32,768 and return incorrect calculations.

This is why this variable is created as a long.

8.6 Sketch: data logging directly into MS excel

The entire sketch that will data log temperature and humidity measurements from the DHT11 and write the measurements directly into excel is here:

```
#include <SimpleDHT.h>
SimpleDHT11 dht11;
byte temperature;
byte humidity;
```

```
float TimeAve_sec = 60;
int iDelay_msec = 1500;
int pinDHT11 = 4;

long iSaveEvery_min = 10;

float TimeNow_hrs;
long iTimeLastSave_msec;
long iTimeStart_msec;

int nptsAve = TimeAve_sec * 1000 / iDelay_msec;
float tempAve_degC;
float humidAve_rh;

void setup() {

  pinMode(13, OUTPUT);
  pinMode(12, OUTPUT);
  Serial.begin(2000000);
  Serial.println("CLEARSHEET");
  Serial.print("LABEL, Date, Time, TimeNow(hrs),");
  Serial.println("Temperature, Humidity");
  iTimeStart_msec = millis();
  iTimeLastSave_msec=millis();
}

void loop() {
  tempAve_degC = 0.0;
  humidAve_rh = 0.0;
  for (int i = 1; i <= nptsAve; i++) {
    digitalWrite(13, HIGH);
    dht11.read(pinDHT11, &temperature, &humidity, NULL);
    digitalWrite(13, LOW);
    tempAve_degC = tempAve_degC + temperature;
    humidAve_rh = humidAve_rh + humidity;
    delay(iDelay_msec);
  }
  digitalWrite(12, HIGH);
  TimeNow_hrs = 0.001 * (millis() - iTimeStart_msec) / 3600.0;
  tempAve_degC = tempAve_degC / nptsAve;
  humidAve_rh = humidAve_rh / nptsAve;

  Serial.print("DATA, DATE"); Serial.print(", ");
  Serial.print("TIME"); Serial.print(", ");
  Serial.print(TimeNow_hrs, 3); Serial.print(", ");
  Serial.print(tempAve_degC); Serial.print(", ");
  Serial.print(humidAve_rh);
  digitalWrite(12, LOW);

  if (millis() > (iTimeLastSave_msec + iSaveEvery_min * 60 * 1000)) {
    Serial.print(", ");  Serial.println("saved");
    Serial.println("SAVEWORKBOOK");
    iTimeLastSave_msec = millis();
  }
  else {
```

```
      Serial.println("");
    }
}
```

My final code above, implements a few special features to facilitate data logging:

- *using the blue LED to show when data is being taken*
- *averaging a number of consecutive data points to get lower noise*
- *data logging directly into excel*
- *plotting the data as we take it in excel*
- *saving the excel workbook periodically*
- *printing a save icon at every time stamp when the file is saved*

These features can be used over and over again in other experiments.

Using this final code, we can take data for extended periods and have confidence it will be saved. Figure 8.6 shows an example of the final, saved spreadsheet, recording the temperature and humidity in my house, over a ten-hour period.

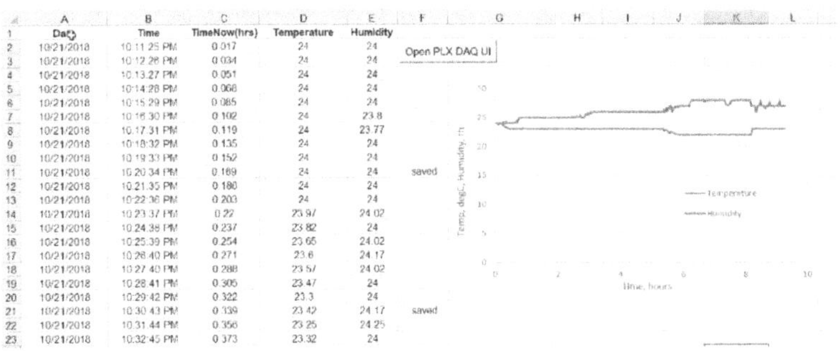

	A	B	C	D	E	F
1	Date	Time	TimeNow(hrs)	Temperature	Humidity	
2	10/21/2018	10:11:25 PM	0.017	24	24	Open PLX DAQ UI
3	10/21/2018	10:12:26 PM	0.034	24	24	
4	10/21/2018	10:13:27 PM	0.051	24	24	
5	10/21/2018	10:14:28 PM	0.068	24	24	
6	10/21/2018	10:15:29 PM	0.085	24	24	
7	10/21/2018	10:16:30 PM	0.102	24	23.8	
8	10/21/2018	10:17:31 PM	0.119	24	23.77	
9	10/21/2018	10:18:32 PM	0.135	24	24	
10	10/21/2018	10:19:33 PM	0.152	24	24	
11	10/21/2018	10:20:34 PM	0.169	24	24	saved
12	10/21/2018	10:21:35 PM	0.186	24	24	
13	10/21/2018	10:22:36 PM	0.203	24	24	
14	10/21/2018	10:23:37 PM	0.22	23.97	24.02	
15	10/21/2018	10:24:38 PM	0.237	23.82	24	
16	10/21/2018	10:25:39 PM	0.254	23.65	24.02	
17	10/21/2018	10:26:40 PM	0.271	23.6	24.17	
18	10/21/2018	10:27:40 PM	0.288	23.57	24.02	
19	10/21/2018	10:28:41 PM	0.305	23.47	24	
20	10/21/2018	10:29:42 PM	0.322	23.3	24	
21	10/21/2018	10:30:43 PM	0.339	23.42	24.17	saved
22	10/21/2018	10:31:44 PM	0.356	23.25	24.25	
23	10/21/2018	10:32:45 PM	0.373	23.32	24	

Figure 8.6. An example of the result of the final version of this code which plots the data as it comes in and is saved periodically. This data is the temperature and humidity in my home over a ten-hour period.

In this example, we also see in the F column, the recording of when the file was most recently saved. This just makes it easier to keep track of what is going on under the hood. This is a valuable diagnostic of the performance of the sketch.

This example also illustrates the power of data logging with a time and date stamp. The data is already saved in an excel spreadsheet and the plot can be monitored as the data is taken.

8.7 Alternatives to PLX-DAQ v2

This software is really a macro running in Microsoft Excel. The downside is, it only runs on a PC and requires excel.

If you don't have both of these, you can't use PLX-DAQ v2. There are a number of alternative software tools written in processing or python, both free tools, that will record the data and plot them. Most of them just record the data and place them in a file for later import into a spreadsheet.

But this is exactly what the terminal program YAT, described in the last chapter, does. If you want to record the measurements into a file and import this data into your favorite spreadsheet, use YAT.

If you want to do one step beyond what the serial plotter can do, and basically turn you Arduino into a data logging strip chart recorded, there is a commercial tool that will do this for you. At $40 for a license, it is not cheap, but is very effective.

The tool is MakerPlot. It only runs on a PC, but basically turns your Arduino into the front end of a flexible data acquisition system. Not only can it read the analog and digital pins and plot the values in real time, it can store the data to a file and even send signals back to the Arduino over the serial com link to have it make changes. Figure 8.7 shows an example of a screen shot from MakerPlot.

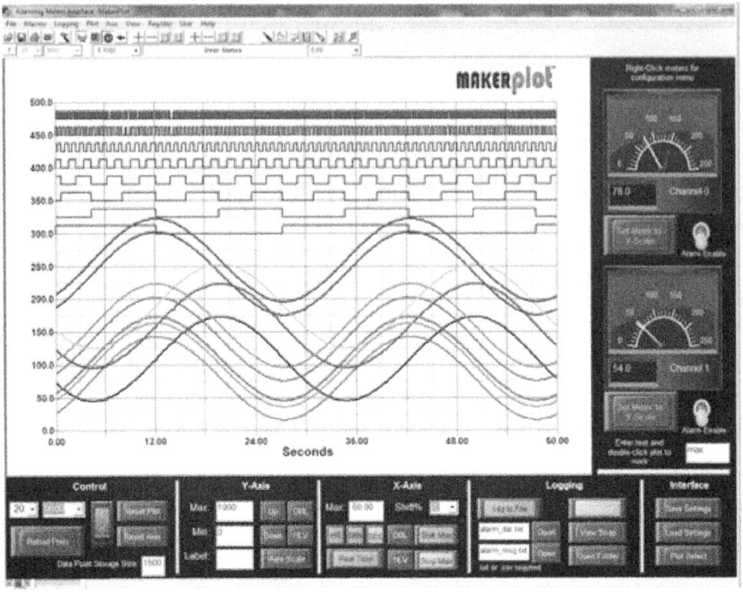

Figure 8.7. An example of the display features of MakerPlot for both analog and digital signals.

While relatively expensive, this software tool will allow you plot the measurements, analyze the results and responds to the measurements either on the Arduino or on your PC.

8.8 Summary of the commands introduced so far

Command	Description

void setup (){
 	
}
	This is a function that appears in EVERY sketch. Every command within the brackets will be executed just once

void loop (){
 	
}
	This is a function that appears in EVERY sketch. Every command within the brackets will execute over and over again.

`pinMode(13, OUTPUT);`	This command tells the Arduino that we are going to use a specific digital pin as an OUTPUT, as distinct from an INPUT. We use the pin number to identify the pin we want to setup.
`digitalWrite(13, HIGH);`	This command controls the output of a digital pin and makes it either a HIGH (logic 1, or 5 V) or a LOW (a logic 0 or a 0 V). Once executed, the pin value will be set to this value.
`delay(1000);`	This command for tell the Arduino to sit there, twiddling its thumbs, doing nothing for a duration of milliseconds as listed inside the (). In this example, the time interval to wait is 1000 msec = 1 sec.
// or /* */	Everything after these two forward slashes will be ignored by the Arduino sketch. We can use this add comments for our own benefit on any line. For multiple lines add them between the /* and the */ lines.
delayMicroseconds(1000);	Just like the delay() function, this function will force the Arduino to sit there and do nothing, for a time duration equal to the time, in microseconds inside the (). In this examples, 1000 microseconds = 1 msec = 0.001 sec.
`Serial.begin(9600);`	This command opens up the serial com link with a baud rated inside the (). In this example the baud rate is 9600 baud. The name Serial is an object, the serial link. The .begin is a verb, telling the object to get set up.

`Serial.print("Hello World");`	This command will print characters to the serial communications channel. Everything inside the () will be printed. To print a string, enclose the characters within quotes. After printing, the cursor will be left on the same line.
`Serial.println(" ");`	Does the same thing as the `Serial.print` command, but moves the cursor to the next line after printing the characters.
`int`	We use this to assign a variable name as a new variable. It is place at the beginning of the sketch. We have to assign a variable name to a type of variable. This command creates a variable that is a + or – whole number up to 2^{15} = 32, 767
`long`	This assigns a variable name to a + and – whole number up to 2^31 = 2,147, 483, 647. Use this when we expect to be counting very large number. You can never go wrong making all integer variables Long variable.
`float`	This assigns a variable as a floating-point number, which is any number having a decimal point. Use this command when the variable needs to have a decimal point.

`for (int i = 1; i <= 10; i++) {`
`  //execute this code if i<=10`
`}`
	This is a loop that causes all the code within the { and } brackets to execute for a certain number of times. Inside the () of the command are three sections, separated by ;. The first sets up the index that will step, and its initial value. The second, sets up the condition. While this is true the loop continues. When it is false, the loop breaks to after the }. The last section increments the index, i, by 1.

`sin(Phase_rad)`	This function returns the value of the sine of the number inside the (), assuming this number is an angle in radians. 2 x π radians = 360 deg.
digitalRead(5)	This command will read the digital value of the pin number inside the (), 5, in this example, and return the value as a 0 or 1 or false or true. Once executed, this command becomes the value it reads.
millis()	This function returns the value of the internal counter which is counting the number of milliseconds since the beginning of the sketch. Nothing is placed inside the (). This is a long integer. Every time it is called, it becomes the current value of milliseconds.
micros()	This function returns the value of the internal timer, which is counting up microseconds since the start of the sketch. The resolution is 4 microseconds. Nothing is placed inside the (). This is a long integer. Every time it is called, it becomes the current value of microseconds.

while (i>1) { }	This command will cause all the code within the {…} to execute over and over again, as long as the condition inside the (…) is true.
random(min, max);	This command returns a random integer value that is between the min value and the (max-1) value. The random number returned is a long integer.
#include <SimpleDHT.h>	The include command tells the Arduino to go to the list of libraries you have installed using the library manager and grab the one identified in the <…>. Then add all the commands listed in this library to the commands available for this sketch. It's like we are adding some new vocabulary words to what the Arduino understands.
SimpleDHT11 dht11(pinDHT11);	The command, SimpleDHT11 is a specific command in the library we included in the previous statement. It tells the Arduino to create a new object, called dht11. The number in the () is the value of the digital pin that is connected to the DHT11 sensor. Once this object is created, we can make it do things by appending verbs to its end separated by a period.

Chapter 9. Measure and Display Your Heartbeat

In this experiment, we are going to take advantage of a trick to monitor our blood pulsing through our finger.

The technique is called *photoplethysmography*. It basically relies on the fact that when blood flows through a finger or an earlobe, the thickness of your veins increases and decreases as your blood ebbs and flows. This changes the transparency or reflectivity of your finger. This is the basic method used in many watch based heart monitors such as the Apple iWatch.

You will measure the light intensity transmitted through your finger. As the blood flow in your finger increases and decreases with each contraction of your heart, it will change the light intensity transmitted. This is illustrated in Figure 9.1.

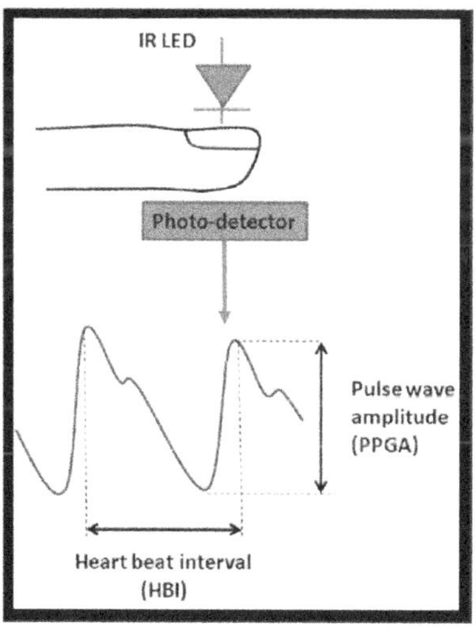

Figure 9.1. An example of measuring the blood flow in your finger with the light that passes through it and the typical light intensity curve.

Generally, the transmitted light will decrease as more blood is flowing in your finger and increase in intensity when less blood flows.

In principle, some colors of light work better than others. Shine a bright flashlight through your finger and it looks red. This is because all except the red colors are absorbed by your finger.

A red LED would be a better light source to use than a green or blue one, for example, since red transmits so well through your finger. But we also want a simple method to implement our heartbeat sensor using just what is available on the multi-function board.

Luckily, there is a small photo-resistor on the multi-function board you can use to measure the light through your finger. You just have to use a bright light as the source.

Any source of bright light will work in this experiment, even room ambient light. But to get the largest change in light intensity due to your blood flow, you want to use as bright a light as you can shine through your finger. The best source is a small battery powered LED flashlight, but any bright light, like a lamp, will do.

9.1 Printing ADC values to the serial monitor averaged for a time period

One way of creating a strip chart recorder is to use the same routine we did when we first started taking measurements: just do a

```
Serial.println(analogRead(A0));
```

command, in a loop, print the measurements as quickly as possible to the serial link, and plot them on the serial plotter as they come in.

When we do this, it's too fast to see clearly.

How fast is it? We can use the same routine we introduced in an earlier experiment when we measured the execution tome of any operation.

We use the same method to measure the time it takes to record an ADC value and print it over the serial port.

Here is the sketch to measure the execution time of any operation:

```
float VperADU = 3.3 / 659.25; // Vref_V/Vref_ADU
int pinADC = A5;
long iTimeStart_usec = 0;
float timeOperation_usec;
void setup() {
  Serial.begin(2000000);
}
void loop() {
  float V_ref1_ADU = 0.0;
  iTimeStart_usec = micros();
  for (int i = 1; i <= 10000; i++) {

/// place code here to measure the execution time

    V_ref1_ADU = V_ref1_ADU + analogRead(pinADC) * 1.0;

/// stop execution

  }
  timeOperation_usec = (micros() - iTimeStart_usec) / 10000.0;
  V_ref1_ADU = V_ref1_ADU / 10000.0;
  Serial.println(timeOperation_usec);
}
```

When I set the baud rate to the highest value, 2,000,000, I measured an execution time of 256 usec to record and print an ADC value. This is almost twice as long as the 112 usec it takes to just take a reading of the ADC.

If we reduce the baud rate to 9600, the typically used default baud rate, the time to execute an operation of reading the data and sending the value over the com link, is 5,132 usec, or 5.132 msec. This is about 20x slower with the lower baud rate.

The higher ADC sample and print rate is one reason why you should always use as high a baud rate as is still robust, so you spend less time in the overhead of sending data over the com link, and more time doing whatever it is your sketch is trying to do.

At the highest baud rate, 2,000,000, if we just send every measurement we take over the com link, we will sample data every 256 usec = 0.000256 sec. This is 1/0.000256 sec = 4,000 times per second, too fast for us to see and look for patterns.

The serial plotter screen holds 500 points at any one time. This would fill in 500 points/4,000 points/sec = 0.125 second.

We could slow it down by just adding a delay(10) command in the path. But this wastes the valuable time of the microcontroller having it sit there, literally twiddling its thumbs, when it could be taking measurements and averaging.

In the last chapter, we slowed the display of the measurement by averaging for a fixed number of points. In this next step, we will average for a fixed time interval, and record just the average value and time at which each point was taken.

9.2 Averaging for a time interval

Rather than using a *for loop* to take some number of points and estimate the time it will take for the average, we can actually control the averaging time based on the actual timer information.

The algorithm we want to implement is:

1. *Initialize the appropriate variables.*
2. *Start the timer*
3. *Calculate the timer value for the end of the averaging interval*
4. *If we haven't reached this time yet, take a measurement and add it to the running sum.*
5. *Keep taking measurements and averaging them.*

6. *After we reach the end of the averaging interval, take the running sum and divide by the number of points measured.*
7. *Save the averaged value in ADU and convert it to volts.*
8. *Estimate the time at the center of the acquisition period and print this as the acquisition time.*
9. *Print out:*
    a. *the index number for the point,*
    b. *the number of points averaged*
    c. *the actual time averaged*
    d. *the time instant for the point*
    e. *the average value in mV.*

Try this experiment: At this point, you should be able to write the code to implement this algorithm. We have done each of these steps before. Here's a hint, try using a *while* statement. While the *current* time is less than the calculated *stop* time, keep taking averages. Give it a try.

9.3 Sketch: Averaging ADC measurements over a fixed time interval

Here is the sketch I used:

```
///fill in these numbers///////
float VperADU = 3.3 / 659.25; // Vref_V/Vref_ADU
int pinADC = A0;
float time2Average_msec = 50.0;// time we want to average for

////create these variables:////
float V_V;
float V_ADU;
long index = 0; //index count of each point measured
long nCountsMeasured;// number of actual measurements averaged
```

```
long iTimeStart_usec; // start of averaging time
long iTimeStop_usec; // stop of averaging time
float timeMeas_sec; // the measurement instant for each averaged value
long iTimeBegin_usec; // the beginning of the sketch
long iTimeAverageActual_usec;// actual amount of time averaged

void setup() {
  Serial.begin(2000000);
  iTimeBegin_usec = micros(); //begin sketch clock
}
void loop() {
  ////initialize variables at start of loop///
  index++;
  V_ADU = 0.0;
  nCountsMeasured = 0;
  iTimeStart_usec = micros();
  iTimeStop_usec = iTimeStart_usec + time2Average_msec * 1000 - 112 / 2;
  ///// 112/2 is to round up to the nearest sample point

  while (micros() < iTimeStop_usec) {
    V_ADU = V_ADU + analogRead(pinADC) * 1.0;
    nCountsMeasured++;
  }

  iTimeAverageActual_usec = micros() - iTimeStart_usec;
  V_V = (V_ADU * 1.0) / nCountsMeasured * VperADU;
  timeMeas_sec = micros() - iTimeBegin_usec;
  timeMeas_sec = timeMeas_sec-0.5*(micros()-iTimeStart_usec);
  timeMeas_sec=TimeMeas_sec *1.0e-6;

  //////////////print out the terms////////
  Serial.print(index); Serial.print(",  ");
  Serial.print(nCountsMeasured); Serial.print(",  ");
  Serial.print(iTimeAverageActual_usec); Serial.print(",  ");
  Serial.print(timeMeas_sec, 6); Serial.print(",  ");
  Serial.println(V_V * 1000.0, 3);
}
```

I demonstrate seven useful tricks in this sketch:

1. *There will be some variables for which we will assign their values. I find putting them at the very top of the sketch makes it so much easier to see them and change their values.*

2. *To have the fastest execution, don't perform a calculation in the conditional comparison of the while loop. Perform the calculation before the while statement.*

3. *Always use the fastest baud rate to reduce the overhead time for printing and communication.*

4. *The vertical resolution of the serial plotter is no smaller than 6 units full scale. With the averaging, we might see a change in each measured point smaller than even 1 ADU. To be able to plot these small changes, we plot the value of the voltage measured, in units of mV. This allows a higher resolution as each integer value plotted corresponds to a 1 mV change.*

5. *While I try to use variable names that are self-documenting, including their units in the variable name, I also add comments to describe the variable when I create it.*

6. *I use commented lines to break up the code into sections to make it easier to see the flow.*

7. *To break up long lines, I try to put pieces of the calculations on one line and just continue the calculation on the next line.*

When this sketch executes, it prints out five columns of data:

- *the index value of each point*
- *number of measurements averaged*
- *actual averaging time in usec*
- *the instant in time for each measurement, in sec*
- *the averaged measured voltage, in mV*

An example of a section of the printout, using an averaging time of 50 msec is shown in Figure 9.2

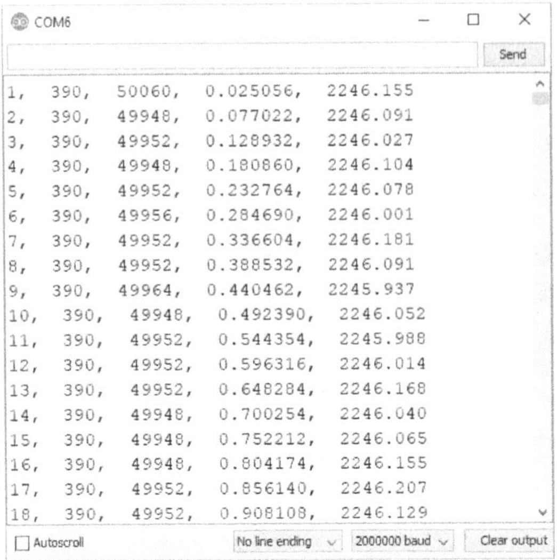

Figure 9.2. Example of the serial monitor print out for these five columns of data.

We set the averaging time as 50.0 msec. The actual averaging time ranges from 49.048 msec to 49.964. This is a variation of about 900 usec. There are 390 measurements taken in each average.

The time between successive points is not every 50 msec, though. The difference in time between consecutive values in the fourth column is about 51.9 msec. This means there is about 1.9 msec of overhead taken up in the calculations and the printing of the columns.

When five columns of data are printed to the serial com channel, a total of 38 characters, including the spaces and commas, are transmitted. This takes 1.9 msec. This means the overhead time to print one character is 1.9 msec/ 38 characters = 0.05 msec per character.

If we are only plotting the voltage values to the serial plotter, this is typically 8 characters, including the decimal point. The time it will take to transmit these characters should be only 8 characters x 0.05 msec/character = 0.4 msec.

This suggests that the actual time between successive data measurements will be the selected averaging time + 0.4 msec.

For example, if we want exactly 60 msec between measurements, we should actually use an averaging time of 60 msec - 0.4 msec = 59.6 msec.

With 500 points displayed, this would be 500 x 60 msec/point = 30000 msec = 30 second full screen.

To test this calibration, I used a function generator (described in another eBook in this series) to generate a sine wave with a period of exactly 30 second. This means that if the serial plotter time interval is 30 seconds, we should see exactly one cycle of the sine wave in the interval at any instant.

Whatever voltage the sine wave started on at the beginning of the interval, it will stop on exactly 1 cycle later, at the end of the interval. Figure 9.3 shows exactly this behavior. I set the averaging interval as 60 – 0.4 msec and measured the 0.03333 Hz sine wave on the A3 pin of the Arduino.

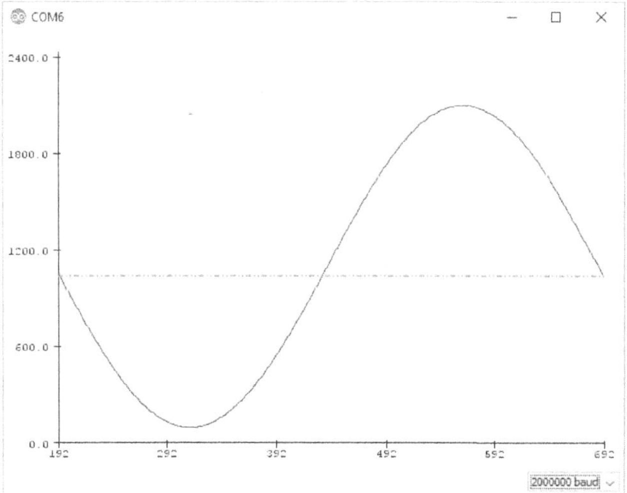

Figure 9.3. Measured sine wave with period of exactly 30 seconds. The starting voltage is at the same level as the ending voltage. This confirms the calibration of the time base.

9.4 What's a good averaging time?

There are two important criteria to decide the best averaging time.

The first is the ***time resolution*** we want to measure.

If we are looking at something that changes slowly over a few seconds, then averaging for 0.1 second might be just fine. If we are looking at something that varies over a few msec, then averaging for 100 msec will completely hide what we are looking for.

If we are not sure of how fast we expect our signal to change, then we may have to just experiment.

The second criterion the averaging time influences is the ***total time displayed*** on the serial plotter at one time.

There are 500 points displayed. If the interval between measurements is 0.1 second, the total time displayed at any instant is 500 x 0.1 sec = 50 seconds. The connection between total time displayed and averaging time is:

$$\text{TotalTime} = 500 \times (\text{aveTime} + 0.4\ \text{msec}) \backslash *$$

MERGEFORMAT (1.1)

Or

$$\text{aveTime} = \frac{\text{TotalTime}}{500} - 0.4\ \text{msec} \backslash *$$

MERGEFORMAT (1.2)

For example, if we want a total time displayed of 60 seconds, we would use an averaging time of 60 sec/500 – 0.4 msec = 120 msec – 0.4 msec = 119.6 msec.

Likewise, a 30 second window displayed at any one time would require an averaging time of 30 sec/500 – 0.4 msec = 60 msec – 0.4 msec = 59.6 msec.

9.5 Two examples

The multi-function board comes with three analog sensors:

A0 is a resistor pot

A1 is a photoresistor

A2 is a temperature sensor.

Unfortunately, in every multifunction board I have measured, the LM35 temperature sensor connected to pin A2 has not worked. This seems to be an issue with the LM35. I purchased a dozen of these units and none of them worked either.

This leaves two built-in analog sensors.

On A0 is the resistor pot. Turning the knob changes the voltage on pin A0. Figure 9.4 is an example of the measured voltage on the pot as it was varied over the full scale of 0 V to 5 V. The averaging time per point was 60 msec – 0.4 msec for a total time displayed of 30 seconds.

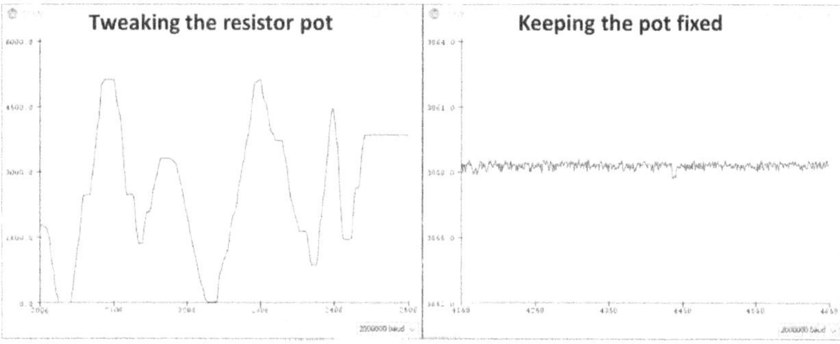

Figure 9.4. Measured voltage on the resistor pot with 30 seconds displayed in each window. Left: scale is 1.5 V per div. Right: with the resistor fixed in position, a measure of the noise, on a scale of 3 mV/div.

When the pot is stationary, the voltage is not changing. This is a measure of the noise level and how small a change in voltage could be measured.

In this example, with the pot stationary, the noise is less than 0.5 mV peak to peak. This is incredible considering the digital resolution of the ADC is 5 mV. The lower noise is primarily due to the averaging.

The second sensor is the photo resistor. With lights shining in the room, the voltage across it was measured as about 1.23 V. It gets higher when the light gets brighter.

An example of the measured voltage on the photo resistor is shown in Figure 9.5. Because the noise level is less than 1 mV peak to peak, and the photo resistor is sensitive to light, we can measure very small changes. These can be created by very small changes in how the shadows interact with the photo resistor.

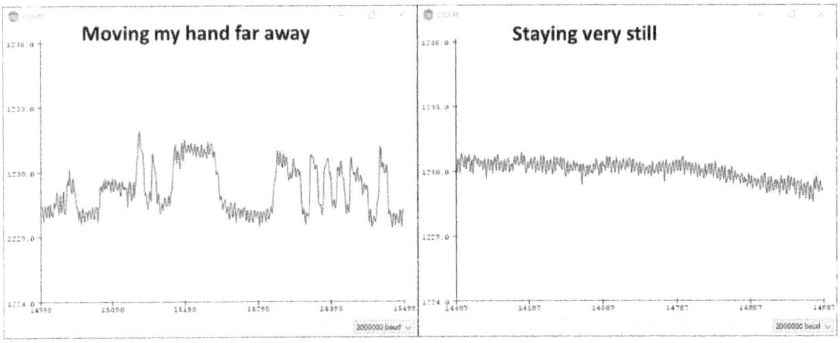

Figure 9.5. Measured voltage across the photo resistor. The time base is 30 seconds full scale in both examples. Left: sensitive to small motions far from the sensor. Right: the noise floor, staying very still. Both vertical scales are 3 mV/div.

Using this simple averaging method, it's possible to measure very small changes in the light levels. This could be used as a motion detector.

Try this experiment: Using the code in this chapter, what is the smallest light level change you can see. How far away from the sensor can you still see your motion?

9.6 The photo-resistor

To measure the light intensity through your finger, we need a sensor that responds to light intensity. This is the photo-resistor built into the multi-function board. This sensor is shown in Figure 9.6

Figure 9.6. The photoresistor sensor on the multi-function board is on the far-right edge.

The resistance of the sensor depends on the light intensity shining on it. When it is dark with little light, the resistance is high, about 250k Ohm. When light shines on it, the resistance can be very low, as low as 10k Ohm. The sensitivity of the resistance to light intensity is very non-linear.

To measure the change in resistance, we have to convert the resistance change into a voltage. We do this using a voltage divider circuit, which is built into the multi-function board.

On the multi-function board is a 10k Ohm resistor in series with the photo resistor. One end of the circuit connects to the 5 V rail while the other end connects to ground. This circuit is shown in Figure 9.7.

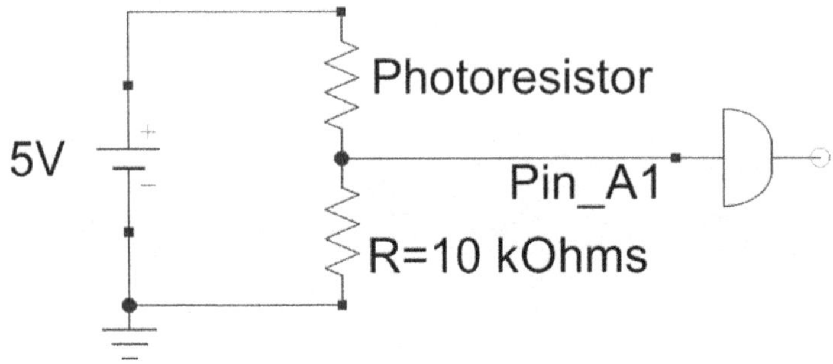

Figure 9.7. Equivalent circuit of the 10k resistor on the board and the photo resistor connected into pin A1.

Ideally, we would like the connection to be arranged so that a brighter light on the photo sensor, which means a lower resistance change, creates a higher voltage at A1. In this circuit, the smaller the resistance of the photo-resistor, the larger the measured voltage, just as we would like.

In this voltage divider circuit, the voltage we measure at the junction point is

$$V\_meas = 5\text{ V}\frac{10k}{(10k + R\_photoresistor)}$$

At its brightest, when the photo-resistor resistance is close to 10k Ohm, we should measure a voltage of about 2.5 V.

At its darkest, when the resistance is 250k Ohms, we should measure a voltage of about

$$V\_meas = 5\text{ V}\frac{10k}{(10k + 250k)} = 0.19\text{ V}$$

9.7 Sketch: measure the voltage across the resistor averaged for 3 power line cycles.

In Experiment #10, we developed a sketch to measure the voltage on an ADC pin, averaged for a number of power line cycles and display the value on the serial plotter, with fixed scales. Here is that sketch, set to measure the A1 pin for 3 PLCs.:

```
///fill in these numbers///////
float VperADU = 3.3 / 659.25; // Vref V/Vref_ADU
int pinADC = A1;
int nPLC = 1;
float time2Average_msec = 1000.0 * nPLC / 60.0;
// time we want to average for
//float time2Average_msec = 1.0;//time for which we want to average
////create these variables:////
float V_V;
float V_ADU;
long index = 0; //index count of each point measured
long nCountsMeasured;// number of actual measurements averaged
long iTimeStart_usec; // start of averaging time
long iTimeStop_usec; // stop of averaging time
float timeMeas_sec; // the measurement instant for each averaged value
long iTimeBegin_usec; // the beginning of the sketch
long iTimeAverageActual_usec;// actual amount of time averaged

void setup() {
  Serial.begin(2000000);
  iTimeBegin_usec = micros(); //begin sketch clock
}
void loop() {
  ////initialize variables at start of loop///
  index++;
  V_ADU = 0.0;
  nCountsMeasured = 0;
  iTimeStart_usec = micros();
  iTimeStop_usec = iTimeStart_usec + time2Average_msec * 1000 + 112 / 2;
  ///// 112/2 is to round up to the nearest sample point

  while (micros() < iTimeStop_usec) {
    V_ADU = V_ADU + analogRead(pinADC) * 1.0;
    nCountsMeasured++;
  }

  iTimeAverageActual_usec = micros() - iTimeStart_usec;
  V_V = (V_ADU * 1.0) / nCountsMeasured * VperADU;
  timeMeas_sec = (micros() - iTimeBegin_usec - 0.5 * (micros() - iTimeStart_usec)) / 1.0e6;

  //////////////print out the terms////////
  //  Serial.print(index); Serial.print(",  ");
  //  Serial.print(nCountsMeasured); Serial.print(",  ");
  //  Serial.print(iTimeAverageActual_usec); Serial.print(",  ");
  //  Serial.print(timeMeas_sec, 6); Serial.print(",  ");
  Serial.println(V_V * 1000.0, 3);

  ////plot with fixed scales
  //  Serial.print(V_V * 1000.0, 3); Serial.print(",");
  //  Serial.print(0); Serial.print(",");
  //  Serial.println(800);
}
```

I commented out the fixed scale print lines at the bottom and turned on the print line for the output voltage in mV. This will allow the serial plotter to auto-scale. This sketch is set to average for 1 PLCs.

With 1 power line cycle average, the time per point is 17 msec. With 500 points full scale, this is a time scale of 0.017 sec x 500 points = 8.5 seconds full scale on the horizontal axis.

When I did this experiment, I moved the sensor close to a lamp and then moved it into the shadows and covered it with my finger. The recordings are shown in Figure 9.8.

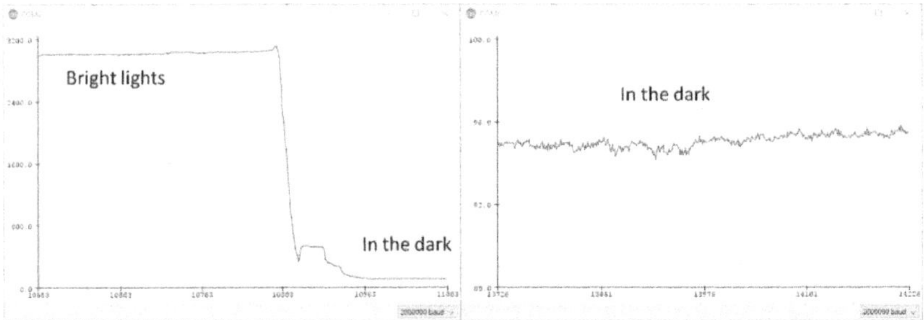

Figure 9.8. Measured voltage on pin A1, across the 10-k resistor of the photoresistor when bright and when dark. The second plot on the right is when the sensor was in the dark. The vertical scale is the measured voltage in mV.

We expected to see about 2.5 V when bright and 0.19 V when dark. We actually measured about 3.0 V when bright and 0.096 V when dark. These are close to what we expected to see.

9.8 Sensitivity of the photo-resistor

Even though the photo-resistor is not linear, we can still use it to measure very small changes in light intensity.

While experimenting with the sensor, I had placed a small piece of paper over the light sensor. When I accidentally tapped the paper, it bounced ever so slightly, changing the light intensity that hit the sensor. This was recorded as small oscillations, as shown in Figure 9.9

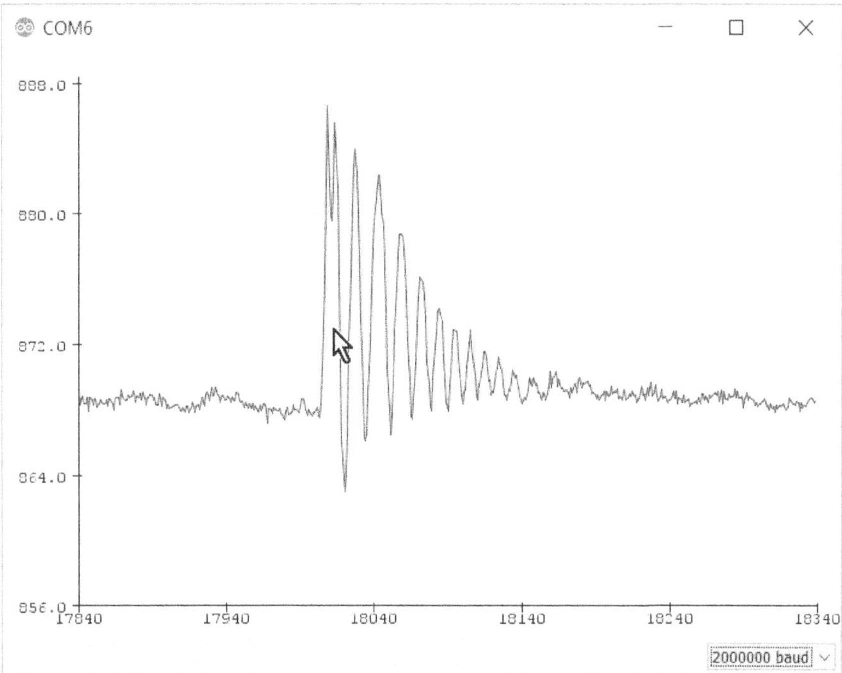

Figure 9.9. An example of the sensitivity of the photo sensor to small changes in light intensity. I tapped a piece of paper over the sensor. We see the rocking of the paper. The vertical scale is in mV.

This demonstrates that we are able to measure small changes in the light intensity. The oscillation amplitude starts with an amplitude of about 20 mV peak-to-peak out of a total signal of 880 mV. This is about a 2% change.

When the light intensity is nearly constant, we can measure just how small a change in voltage it's possible to measure.

Try this experiment. Keeping the sensor still and not moving, how stable a voltage can you measure when the light intensity on the photo-resistor is not changing?

When I did this experiment, I was able to record the voltage on the photo-resistor as shown in Figure 9.10. The variation is about 1 mV peak-to-peak. This is out of a signal of about 1125 mV, or a little less than 0.1% peak to peak change.

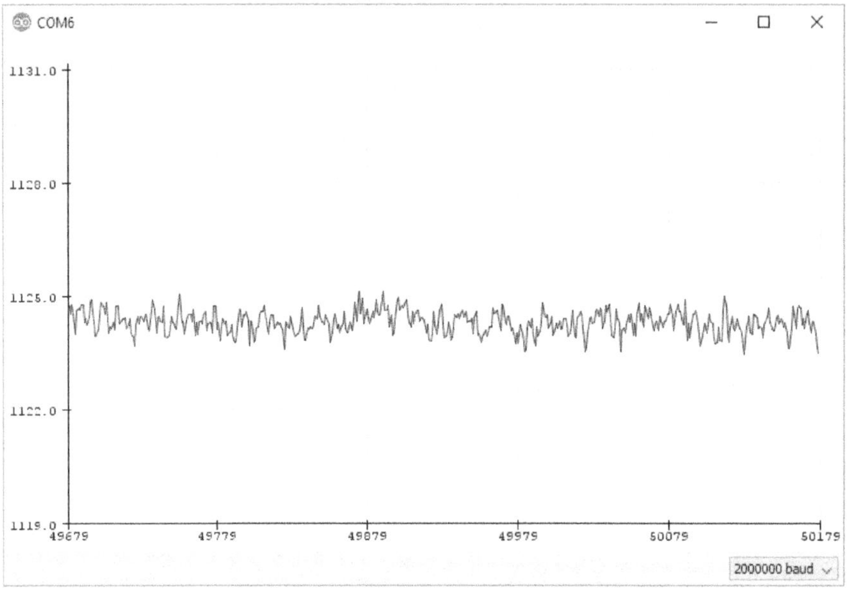

Figure 9.10. Measured photoresistor signal in room light, with no motion. The signal was 1125 mV. The noise was about 1 mV peak to peak. This is stable to about 0.1%.

9.9 Measuring your heartbeat

Using our averaging method, we have developed a remarkably sensitive light sensor. It can detect changes in the light intensity that are less than 0.1%. And, through these simple experiments, we've convinced ourselves it is indeed very sensitive.

We can take advantage of this to measure the very small light intensity changes at the detector from light passing through our finger.

If we place our finger firmly over the sensor, the only way light will get to the sensor is by passing through our finger. And, as the blood flow changes through our finger, the light intensity to the sensor will be modulated and we will see that change.

Try this experiment: Place your index finger firmly over the photo sensor and hold it under a bright lamp, keeping your hand very steady. Resting your hand on a table so it does not move is very important.

Look for pulses that happen about 60 times a minute or once a second. Using 1 PLC, the time span of the serial plotter is 8.5 seconds. You should see about 8-10 cycles displayed on the screen at any time.

An example of my heartbeat is shown in Figure 9.11.

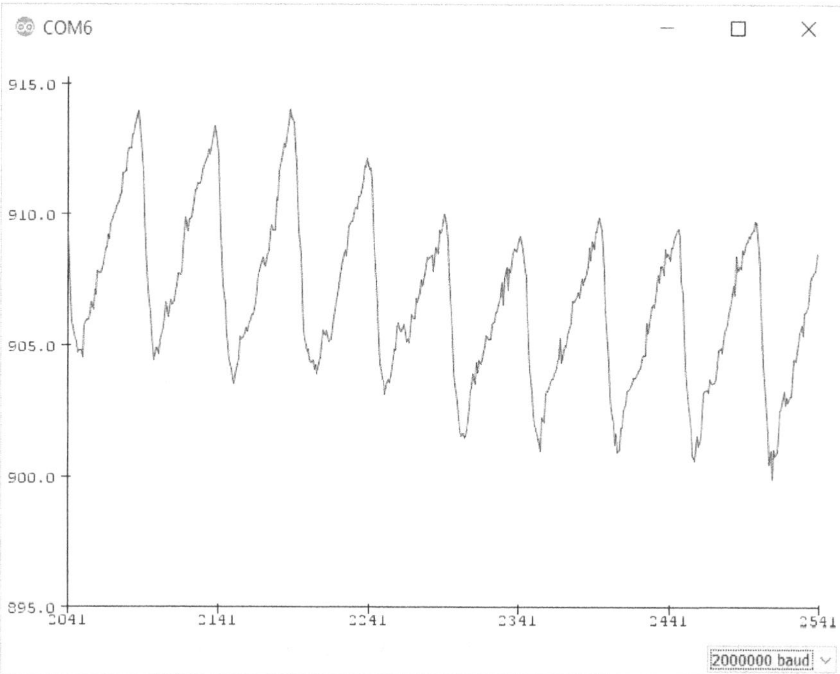

Figure 9.11. The blood flow through my finger. Note the variation is only about 10 mV out of 900 mV or about 1.1% peak to peak modulation!

In this example, there were about 10 pulses in the 8.5 sec total acquisition time. This is about:

$$\frac{10\text{ pulses}}{8.5\text{ sec}} \times \frac{60\text{ sec}}{1\text{min}} = 71\text{pulses / min}$$ * MERGEFORMAT (1.3)

The brighter the light source we use to shine on top of our finger, the stronger the light reaching the sensor will be and the larger the change due to the blood flow through our finger.

In this case, the light intensity created a voltage in the voltage divider circuit of about 900 mV and the modulation by the blood flow in my finger was about 10 mV peak to peak.

The fact we can easily see this 1% peak to peak change is an indication of how sensitive our measurement system is.

9.10 Feedback- a throbbing LED

Now we have a way of sensing our heartbeat. Let's use this to modulate a red LED's intensity so that it throbs to our heartbeat.

Before we set up this experiment, think about how you would implement it. The signal we will be measuring is a very small change, like 1%, in a large value. We want this small change to modulate the LED.

Here is the flow of execution we would follow:

1. *Measure the voltage on the light sensor*
2. *Calculate the average of the last set of measurements*
3. *Subtract the average from the current value*
4. *Using a scale of 0 to 255, assign a value to the current value of blood flow*

5. *Print this to the LED and to the serial plotter*
6. *Repeat*

The challenge here is calculating the running average. In order to average the last n points, we have to store all of them so that we can throw out the old one and add in the new ones. The only way to do this easily is using an array.

9.11 New Code: an array variable

So far, we have identified three types of variables we can use:

- *An int*
- *A long*
- *A float*

Each of these represents a single number. It is 28 or 94.328 or 96,329,288. There is a special type of variable which can represent a series of numbers called an array.

An array is like a column of numbers in a spreadsheet. Each number has a location in each cell, starting with the first cell moving down to the nth cell. We call the location in the array, the *index value*, just a whole number starting at 0 and counting up.

The *content* of each index location is the *element value*. We can have arrays make up of *int* type numbers, *long* type number or *float* type numbers. But every element value has to be the same type. We can't mix and match.

An example of an array filled with float type numbers is shown in Figure 9.12.

1	0.518
2	0.952
3	0.093
4	0.653
5	0.179
6	0.383
7	0.488
8	0.273
9	0.619
10	0.591
11	0.842
12	0.141
13	0.210
14	0.235
15	0.449
16	0.951
17	0.140
18	0.117
19	0.702
20	0.278

Figure 9.12. An array of 20 numbers. Each cell has an index location, in the left column, and a value in that index location, in the right column.

An array takes up memory space in the Arduino. There is a limit to how large an array size we can create. If we use a float type number in each element, a safe number is 301 elements. You can experiment to see how many elements you can create in your array before you get an *out of memory* error.

You will see the error when you try to upload the sketch. If I try to make the array size 501 elements, the out of memory error is shown in Figure 9.13

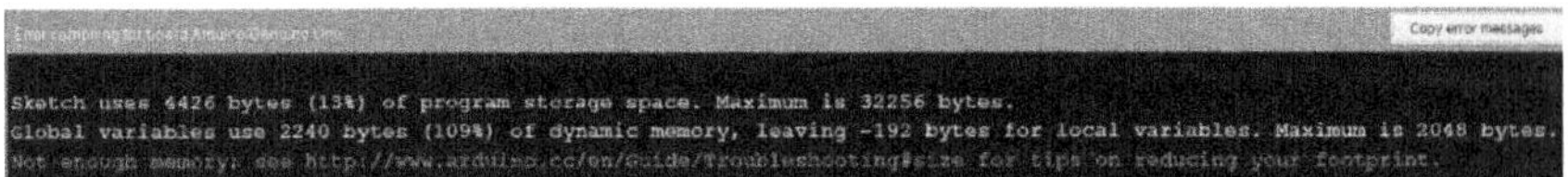

Figure 9.13. The error message you will get if you try to declare an array with more elements that there is room for in the tiny brain of the Atmega 328 microcontroller.

If you want to create an array with more than about 301 elements, you will have to use a more advanced Arduino microcontroller with more memory.

In other eBooks in this series, we introduce more advanced Arduinos that have much more memory. These can all handle arrays as large as 10,000 elements. These are microcontrollers with many more advanced capabilities we will use for the advanced projects in these eBooks but are more expensive.

The syntax to create and use an array of numbers is first to create or declare the array at the beginning. There are a few different ways, but the simplest is to define the type of number in the array and the size, like:

```
float arrV_mV[301];
```

This line, placed before the void setup() function, would create the array variable, arrV_mV and allocate 301 elements for it.

As a habit, I like to name all my array variables with the letters, “arr” in front of the name to remind myself this variable is an array. The rest of the name, V_mV tells me I am storing voltage information in this array and the units of the numbers in each index location is in mV.

The index labeling of each element in an array starts with 0. I find this a little confusing sometimes, so I generally ignore the first element, labeled as index 0 and just use the elements with index values of 1 to 300. All together there are 301 points, when we include the index 0 location.

Inside the brackets, [], when we declare the array variable is the total number of elements in the array, 301 in this case.

To use any element in the array, we simply refer to the value of the element in the indexed location, 12, for example as:

arrV_mV[12] = 42.72;

In this example, we are writing a value in index location, 12, for 42.72. We could also read the value of the element in this location if the array element name were on the other side of the equal sign.

Arrays are great in *for loops* because we can step through all the elements in an array to either write values to the array’s index location or to extract and read the value in that index location. We can access any index location arbitrarily by just using its index value in brackets.

9.12 Calculating a running average

Now comes the secret sauce for using an array to calculate a running average.

In this example, we will use the last 300 points in our running average. Later, we'll make this a variable as well.

This means, at any instant of time we want to calculate the average of the last 300 measurements. The value we display on the serial plotter and use to drive the throbbing LED, will be the current measured value minus this running average, scaled to give us a good range.

1. *The first step is we will collect the first 300 values to fill the array to get us started.*

2. *We then calculate the average of these 300 values.*

3. *We subtract off the average from the current value and scale it*

4. *We use this scaled value to drive the LED and plot the value*

5. *We measure another voltage.*

6. *We shift the value in index location 2 into index location 1. This overwrites the value that was in index location 1 and effectively gets rid of it.*

7. *We continue this process: write the element value in index location 3 into index location 2, all the way up to the 300th element.*

8. *We add the new measurement to this index and start the process over again.*

This is not the most efficient algorithm, but it is very straight forward. We have enough compute power in the tiny Atmega 328 microcontroller chip to do these calculations pretty fast.

Try this experiment:

Given this algorithm, try writing the sketch that implements this algorithm. Instead of using 300 points, use the variable nptsRunningAve.

9.13 Subtracting a running average

Here are a few elements of the final sketch.

The first step is to initialize the array values, so we don't have to wait to take the 300 measurements to fill the array. We will front-load the array with the *initial value.*

The idea is to measure the initial value of the photo resistor voltage. Then we use this value to fill the array to start with. This will give us an initial average very close to the actual measurements.

Here are the variables we introduce:

```
int pinADC = A1;
float arrV_mV[301];
float V_ADU;
int i;
int nptsRunningAve = 100;
float runningAve_mV;
float V_mV;
```

And here is the initial filling of the array, which we do in the void setup() function:

```
analogRead(pinADC); //stabilize the value
delay(2000);
V_ADU = 0;
for (i = 1; i <= 1000; i++) {
   V_ADU = V_ADU + analogRead(pinADC) * 1.0;
 }
```

```
V_mV= (V_ADU / 1000.0) * VperADU * 1000.0;

  for (i = 1; i <= nptsRunningAve; i++) {
    arrV_mV[i] = V_mV;
  }
```

In the first line, we just read the ADC value in the selected pin. This effectively connects the ADC to the input pin we are measuring. Then we wait 2 seconds. This helps to stabilize the value measured in the ADC. If you comment out these lines and run the final sketch, you will see an initial value that takes a little while to stabilize.

After we waited to stabilize the voltage on the ADC pin, the *for loop* will measure the voltage on the ADC pin, over 1000 consecutive measurements. I chose this number of averages arbitrarily. It's large enough to give some averaging, but won't take much time.

We add up 1,000 measurements, each stored as a float number. This way we don't have the round-off error when we add up and then divide by the number of samples to get the average.

Right after this for loop, we calculate the average by dividing the sum of the 1000 measurements by 1000, then turn this ADU value into a voltage and then convert the voltage into mV.

In the second *for loop*, we load this average value, in mV, into each array element.

Once the array is initialized, we go ahead with the same acquisition of each voltage value, averaged over 1 power line cycle. Once we have this value, we now shift the values in the array, add the new value to the last array element, calculate the average, and subtract this off.

Here is the code to shift the elements one row down:

```
///section 5: shift elements one row up
  for (i = 1; i <= nptsRunningAve - 1; i++) {
    arrV_mV[i] = arrV_mV[i + 1];
  }
  arrV_mV[nptsRunningAve] = V_V * 1000.0;
```

In the last line, we place the most recent measurement, in mV, in the last element of the array. The next step is to calculate the running average of the entire array of measurements.

```
///section 6: calc the running average
runningAve_mV = 0.0;
for (i = 1; i <= nptsRunningAve; i++) {
  runningAve_mV = runningAve_mV + arrV_mV[i];
}

runningAve_mV = runningAve_mV / (nptsRunningAve * 1.0);
```

Now that we have the running average, we want to take the last measurement, subtract the running average value from it, and scale this measured voltage, in mV.

The red LED for which we can control the brightness, is connected to digital pin 9. The range of values we can print to pin 9 is only 0 to 255, 8-bit resolution.

We would not expect this measured voltage, after subtracting the average, to be very large. In fact, we can plot these values, along with the running average value to see what its typical amplitude is. Ideally, we want to use a bright light to shine on our finger. This will give us a large signal and a larger modulation.

We print the measured voltage minus the average, and the average value using two simple lines:

```
Serial.print(V_V * 1000.0); Serial.print(",");
Serial.println(runningAve_mV);
```

This will plot the measured value and the running average on the same scale. An example is shown in Figure 9.14.

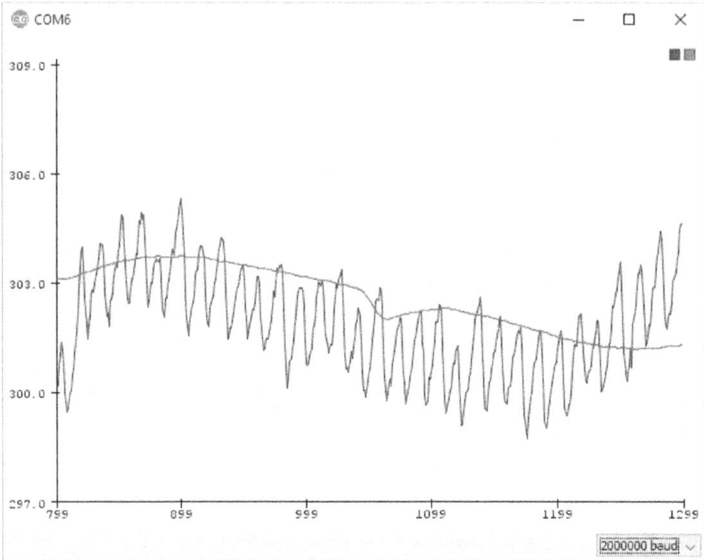

Figure 9.14. An example of the raw, measured light modulation value, showing the heart pulses, and the running average, plotted as the smooth line.

This plot confirms that we are getting a pretty good estimate of the average value. The typical peak to peak value variation is about 7 mV. This is a reasonable value to use to scale the measurements. The variation above and below the average value is 7 mV/2 = ± 3.5 mV.

After we subtract the running average, the average value of the voltage will be 0. On top of this will be the roughly ± 3.5 mV modulation.

We want to turn this modulation into a value from 0 to 255, centered in the middle.

To scale this measurement, we want to first center it about 127, which is the center of the scale.

Next, we want a value of 3.5 mV to scale to 127 ADU units.

The variable we will write to the digital pin 9 is iThrob_ADU

We calculate it as:

iThrob_ADU = (V_V * 1000.0 - runningAve_mV) / 3.5 * 127 + 127;

This is the value that will be sent with the analogWrite () command to pin 9. And, at the same time, we can plot it on the serial plotter using these commands:

```
Serial.println(iThrob_ADU);
analogWrite(9,iThrob_ADU);
```

An example of this plot is shown in Figure 9.15.

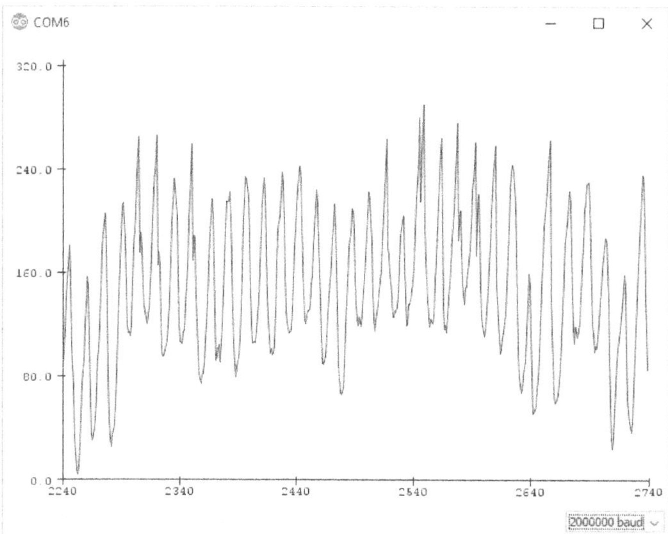

Figure 9.15. An example of the values scale to drive the red LED.

This is the value which will be written to pin 9 and modulate the red led.

One of the terms that will help stabilize the throbbing is the number of points over which we calculate the running average, nptsRunningAve. Experiment with this value. I found a value of about 50 gave the best results. Using this value, the red LED would throb with my heartbeat when I held my finger very steady.

9.14 Sketch: Using your heartbeat to throb a red LED.

The complete sketch to measure the blood flow in your finger, subtract the average off, scale the value and drive a red LED is here:

```
///section 1: fill in these numbers///////
float VperADU = 3.3 / 659.25; // Vref_V/Vref_ADU
int pinADC = A1;
int nPLC = 3;
float time2Average_msec = 1000.0 * nPLC / 60.0; // time we want to average for
//float time2Average_msec = 1.0;//time for which we want to average

////section 2: create these variables:////
float V_V;
float V_mV;
float arrV_mV[301];
float V_ADU;
long index = 0; //index count of each point measured

long nCountsMeasured;// number of actual measurements averaged
long iTimeStart_usec; // start of averaging time
long iTimeStop_usec; // stop of averaging time
float timeMeas_sec; // the measurement instant for each averaged value
long iTimeBegin_usec; // the beginning of the sketch
long iTimeAverageActual_usec;// actual amount of time averaged

int i;
int nptsRunningAve = 50;
float runningAve_mV;
int iThrob_ADU;

void setup() {
  Serial.begin(2000000);


  ///section 3: fill the array with initial values
  analogRead(pinADC); //stabilize the value
  delay(2000);
  V_ADU = 0;
  for (i = 1; i <= 1000; i++) {
    V_ADU = V_ADU + analogRead(pinADC) * 1.0;
  }
  V_mV = (V_ADU / 1000.0) * VperADU * 1000.0;
  for (i = 1; i <= nptsRunningAve; i++) {
    arrV_mV[i] = V_mV;
  }

  ////////////////////////////////////
  iTimeBegin_usec = micros(); //begin sketch clock
}
void loop() {
  ////section 4: measure a voltage over n PLC///
  index++;
  V_ADU = 0.0;
  nCountsMeasured = 0;
  iTimeStart_usec = micros();
  iTimeStop_usec = iTimeStart_usec + time2Average_msec * 1000 - 112 / 2;
  ///// 112/2 is to round up to the nearest sample point

  while (micros() < iTimeStop_usec) {
    V_ADU = V_ADU + analogRead(pinADC) * 1.0;
    nCountsMeasured++;
  }

  iTimeAverageActual_usec = micros() - iTimeStart_usec;
  V_V = (V_ADU * 1.0) / nCountsMeasured * VperADU;
  timeMeas_sec = (micros() - iTimeBegin_usec - 0.5 * (micros() - iTimeStart_usec)) / 1.0e6;

  ///section 5: shift elements one row down
  for (i = 1; i <= nptsRunningAve - 1; i++) {
    arrV_mV[i] = arrV_mV[i + 1];
  }
  arrV_mV[nptsRunningAve] = V_V * 1000.0;

  ///section 6: calc the running average
  runningAve_mV = 0.0;
  for (i = 1; i <= nptsRunningAve; i++) {
    runningAve_mV = runningAve_mV + arrV_mV[i];
  }
  runningAve_mV = runningAve_mV / (nptsRunningAve * 1.0);
  //Serial.print(V_V * 1000.0); Serial.print(",");
```

```
  //Serial.println(runningAve_mV);
  iThrob_ADU = (V_V * 1000.0 - runningAve_mV) / 3.5 * 127 + 127;

  Serial.println(iThrob_ADU);
  analogWrite(9, iThrob_ADU);

  //////////////print out the terms////////
  //    Serial.print(index); Serial.print(",  ");
  //    Serial.print(nCountsMeasured); Serial.print(",  ");
  //    Serial.print(iTimeAverageActual_usec); Serial.print(",  ");
  //    Serial.print(timeMeas_sec, 6); Serial.print(",  ");
  //Serial.println(V_V * 1000.0, 3);
  //Serial.println(iThrob_ADU);

  ////plot with fixed scales
  //  Serial.print(V_V * 1000.0, 3); Serial.print(",");
  //  Serial.print(0); Serial.print(",");
  //  Serial.println(800);
}
```

9.15 Feedback: using the ambient light level to control another light

In this previous example, we used the measured light intensity of the photoresistor to control the light intensity of another LED. This is an example of feedback. Light sensors are often used to monitor the outside light and when it drops too low, to automatically turn on external lights.

On most streetlights, there is a photosensor mounted, facing north, so it does not get the southern sun, which monitors the ambient light. When the light level drops below a set threshold, the streetlight turns on. An example of the sensor mounted to a streetlight in my neighborhood is shown in Figure 9.16.

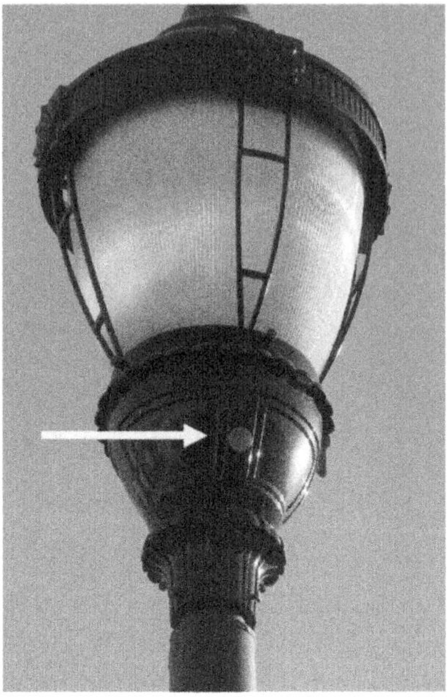

Figure 9.16. Close up of the streetlight showing the small light sensor that automatically turns on the streetlight when the light level drops.

We can use the photo sensor to monitor ambient light and turn on one of the LEDs when the light level gets too low.

If we just use a single threshold to control whether the light is turned off or turned on, we may find when the light level is close to the threshold, the light will fluctuate between off and on and may flicker.

To avoid this problem, we will introduce two different thresholds: a turn-on the light level and a turn-off the light threshold.

Think about how you would implement this algorithm. We'll use the simplest code we can, with no extra averaging.

How would you implement this code? Think about it before you look at my solution.

9.16 Sketch: turning on the lights when it gets too dark

In this sketch, we first print the value of the A1 analog signal that is the photo resistor. This way we can monitor what value is just dark enough to turn on the light.

This value lets determine the iTurnOn_ADU value.

Then, we let the ambient get brighter than this threshold before we turn off the light. This higher value is the iTurnOff_ADU value.

We use the measured light levels as reported to the serial monitor to decide these two thresholds. Then we set them in the code.

My complete code is:

```
int iTurnOn_ADU = 150;
int iTurnOff_ADU = 220;

void setup() {
pinMode(13,OUTPUT);
  Serial.begin(2000000);
}

void loop() {
  Serial.println(analogRead(A1));
  if (analogRead(A1) < iTurnOn_ADU) {
    digitalWrite(13, HIGH);
  }
  if (analogRead(A1) > iTurnOff_ADU) {
    digitalWrite(13, LOW);
  }
}
```

Once we select the values of the thresholds, we can dim the lights and have the blue LED on pin 13 turn on. Then, as the room lights up a little, the light stays on until the room brightens up to the second threshold.

This is how commercial automatic light controllers work.

9.17 Summary of the commands introduced so far

Command	Description

void setup (){
 	
}
	This is a function that appears in EVERY sketch. Every command within the brackets will be executed just once

void loop (){
 	
}
	This is a function that appears in EVERY sketch. Every command within the brackets will execute over and over again.

`pinMode(13, OUTPUT);`	This command tells the Arduino that we are going to use a specific digital pin as an `OUTPUT`, as distinct from an `INPUT`. We use the pin number to identify the pin we want to setup.
`digitalWrite(13, HIGH);`	This command controls the output of a digital pin and makes it either a `HIGH` (logic 1, or 5 V) or a `LOW` (a logic 0 or a 0 V). Once executed, the pin value will be set to this value.
`delay(1000);`	This command for tell the Arduino to sit there, twiddling its thumbs, doing nothing for a duration of milliseconds as listed inside the (). In this example, the time interval to wait is 1000 msec = 1 sec.
// or /* */	Everything after these two forward slashes will be ignored by the Arduino sketch. We can use this add comments for our own benefit on any line. For multiple lines add them between the /* and the */ lines.

delayMicroseconds(1000);	Just like the delay() function, this function will force the Arduino to sit there and do nothing, for a time duration equal to the time, in microseconds inside the (). In this examples, 1000 microseconds = 1 msec = 0.001 sec.
`Serial.begin(9600);`	This command opens up the serial com link with a baud rated inside the (). In this example the baud rate is 9600 baud. The name `Serial` is an object, the serial link. The .`begin` is a verb, telling the object to get set up.
`Serial.print("Hello World");`	This command will print characters to the serial communications channel. Everything inside the () will be printed. To print a string, enclose the characters within quotes. After printing, the cursor will be left on the same line.
`Serial.println(" ");`	Does the same thing as the `Serial.print` command, but moves the cursor to the next line after printing the characters.
`int`	We use this to assign a variable name as a new variable. It is place at the beginning of the sketch. We have to assign a variable name to a type of variable. This command creates a variable that is a + or – whole number up to 2^{15} = 32, 767
`long`	This assigns a variable name to a + and – whole number up to 2^31 = 2,147, 483, 647. Use this when we expect to be counting very large number. You can never go wrong making all integer variables Long variable.

`float`	This assigns a variable as a floating-point number, which is any number having a decimal point. Use this command when the variable needs to have a decimal point.
`Float` Name[100]	Declares an array using the [] to define the number of elements in the array size. Limited to about 301 elements in the Uno

`for (int i = 1; i <= 10; i++) {`
`  //execute this code if i<=10`
`}`
	This is a loop that causes all the code within the { and } brackets to execute for a certain number of times. Inside the () of the command are three sections, separated by ;. The first sets up the index that will step, and its initial value. The second, sets up the condition. While this is true the loop continues. When it is false, the loop breaks to after the }. The last section increments the index, i, by 1.

`sin(Phase_rad)`	This function returns the value of the sine of the number inside the (), assuming this number is an angle in radians. 2 x π radians = 360 deg.
digitalRead(5)	This command will read the digital value of the pin number inside the (), 5, in this example, and return the value as a 0 or 1 or false or true. Once executed, this command becomes the value it reads.
millis()	This function returns the value of the internal counter which is counting the number of milliseconds since the beginning of the sketch. Nothing is placed inside the (). This is a long integer. Every time it is called, it becomes the current value of milliseconds.

`micros()`	This function returns the value of the internal timer, which is counting up microseconds since the start of the sketch. The resolution is 4 microseconds. Nothing is placed inside the (). This is a long integer. Every time it is called, it becomes the current value of microseconds.
`while (i>1) {` `}`	This command will cause all the code within the {…} to execute over and over again, as long as the condition inside the (…) is true.
`random(min, max);`	This command returns a random integer value that is between the min value and the (max-1) value. The random number returned is a long integer.
`#include` `<SimpleDHT.h>`	The include command tells the Arduino to go to the list of libraries you have installed using the library manager and grab the one identified in the <…>. Then add all the commands listed in this library to the commands available for this sketch. It's like we are adding some new vocabulary words to what the Arduino understands.
`SimpleDHT11` `dht11(pinDHT11);`	The command, `SimpleDHT11` is a specific command in the library we included in the previous statement. It tells the Arduino to create a new object, called dht11. The number in the () is the value of the digital pin that is connected to the DHT11 sensor. Once this object is created, we can make it do things by appending verbs to its end separated by a period.

analogRead(pinNumber);	This command will read the ADC channel in the (), as A0, A1,…A5, and return the value as an integer in units of ADUs. The resolution is 10-bit or 1023 different levels. It takes 112 usec to perform one analogRead(pinNumber); operation.

Chapter 10. Can you influence random numbers with your mind?

In the first book in this series, Arduinos Without Tears, we explored random numbers and the random walk pattern. To do this, we created an electronic, random, coin flip.

We were able to create a random sequence of +1 or -1 values. We can use these to decide which color LED to turn on, the red one or the blue one, and then see if we can influence or predict which color will come up.

10.1 Randomly flashing the red or blue LED

We will first build an electronic coin flipper to create a random sequence of red or blue flashing lights. For a refresher on building an electronic coin flipper, review the first book in this series, Arduinos Without Tears.

We can convert the randomly created +1 and -1 values into a red-light flash or a blue-light flash.

Try this experiment: Create a sequence of +1 or -1 values and then convert these into a red or blue light flash. If you get stuck, check out my sketch.

10.2 My sketch to randomly flash a red or blue LED

Here is my sketch to flash the red and blue light randomly.

```
int iRnd;
int iSum;
```

```
int pinBlue = 13;
int pinRed = 12;
int iDelay_msec = 200;

void setup() {
  Serial.begin(2000000);
  pinMode(pinBlue, OUTPUT);
  pinMode(pinRed, OUTPUT);
  randomSeed(micros() + analogRead(A5));
}

void loop() {
  for (int i = 1; i <= 500; i++) {
    iRnd = 2 * random(0, 2) - 1;
    if (iRnd == 1) {
      digitalWrite(pinBlue, HIGH);
      delay(iDelay_msec);
      digitalWrite(pinBlue, LOW);
      delay(iDelay_msec);
    }
    if (iRnd == -1) {
      digitalWrite(pinRed, HIGH);
      delay(iDelay_msec);
      digitalWrite(pinRed, LOW);
      delay(iDelay_msec);
    }
  }
  delay(30000);
}
```

Try this experiment: We have a random LED light flasher. Every flash is a coin flip. Can you influence the coin flip?

Watch the light color. Can you make red come up more often than blue? It may seem that you are getting more reds to come up than blues, but how well does your perception compare to the random walk plot?

Try just looking at the lights flashing and think "red, red, red." At the end of the run, look at the serial plotter display. Are there more reds in this run?

Then press one of the switches to start the next run.

As an alternative, try watching the serial plotter as the random walk is plotted in real time. Can you influence the direction of the random walk? Can you make the plot move to the red lines or the blue lines?

While you are trying to make more reds or more blues, take a look at the random walk plot. Is the result coming up matching a random walk guess?

10.3 Guess the next coin flip: test your *precognition*

In the last experiment, we were informally testing our ability to influence the color that come up. This is a form of telekinesis. It was informal in the sense we just looked at the overall serial plotter to judge our effectiveness.

We can keep better track of each individual trial.

With this random number generator engine we have built, we can perform two types of tests: *telekinesis* and *precognition.*

- ***Precognition**: If the color is selected in the code, and then we guess what color will come up, we are testing how well we can predict the future. This is testing for precognition.*
- ***Telekinesis**: If we guess the color first, then randomly select the color, we are testing how well we can influence the selection. This is a form of telekinesis.*

In this experiment, we want to test the ability of the subject to predict the next color that will flash. This is a test of ***precognition abilities***.

Here are the general steps:

1. *The blue or red color LED will be selected but not turned on, based on a random number being selected.*

2. *The test subject will press the switch under the LED which they think will flash next.*

3. *After the button is pressed, the color actually selected by the random number will flash and the agreement will be recorded.*

4. *A correct prediction is a score of +1 and a wrong prediction is given a score of -1. The cumulative running sum is plotted as a random walk.*

5. *At the end of 500 trials, both LEDs will be turned on and we will wait for a switch to be pressed before continuing the next run.*

There are many ways we can write the code to read the input to a button.

If it were just based on chance, we would expect to correctly predict the red or blue LED will flash 50% of the time. As we saw before, it will not be exactly 50\% but will random walk around 50%. This would be a score of 0 in the cumulative sum.

Try this experiment: How would you write the code to record your prediction and if you predicted the correct color?

10.4 Sketch: predicting the next random number

Here is my code:

```
int iRnd;
int iSum;
int pinBlue = 13;
int pinRed = 12;
int pinSwBlue = 2;
int pinSwRed = 3;
int iDelay_msec = 200;
int iGuess;

void setup() {
  Serial.begin(2000000);
```

```
  pinMode(pinBlue, OUTPUT);
  pinMode(pinRed, OUTPUT);
  pinMode(pinSwBlue, INPUT);
  pinMode(pinSwRed, INPUT);
  randomSeed(micros()+analogRead(A5));
}

void loop() {
  for (int i = 1; i <= 500; i++) {

    //////////////////////////////////////
    iRnd = 2 * random(0, 2) - 1;
    ////////////////////////////////////////

    while ((digitalRead(pinSwBlue) == 1) and (digitalRead(pinSwRed) == 1)) {
    }
    if (digitalRead(pinSwBlue) == 0) {
      iGuess = 1;
    }

    if (digitalRead(pinSwRed) == 0) {
      iGuess = -1;
    }

    if (iRnd == 1) {
      digitalWrite(pinBlue, HIGH);
      delay(iDelay_msec);
      digitalWrite(pinBlue, LOW);
      delay(iDelay_msec);
    }
    if (iRnd == -1) {
      digitalWrite(pinRed, HIGH);
      delay(iDelay_msec);
      digitalWrite(pinRed, LOW);
      delay(iDelay_msec);
    }
    if (iGuess == iRnd) {
      iSum = iSum + 1;
    }

    if (iGuess != iRnd) {
      iSum = iSum - 1;
    }
    Serial.print(sqrt(i)); Serial.print(", ");
    Serial.print(-1 * sqrt(i)); Serial.print(", ");
    Serial.print(2 * sqrt(i)); Serial.print(", ");
    Serial.print(-2 * sqrt(i)); Serial.print(", ");
    Serial.println(iSum);
  }
  delay(30000);
}
```

Remember that the random walk in this experiment is not a plot of the frequency of red or blue flashes, but correct or incorrect guesses.

When the walk goes negative, this means more incorrect guesses. When the walk goes positive, this means more correct guesses.

When I did this test, I found a negative correlation- I guessed wrong more often. Figure 10.1 shows one of my runs. I guessed incorrectly more often. Is my negative correlation significant, or is this what would be expected just based on chance?

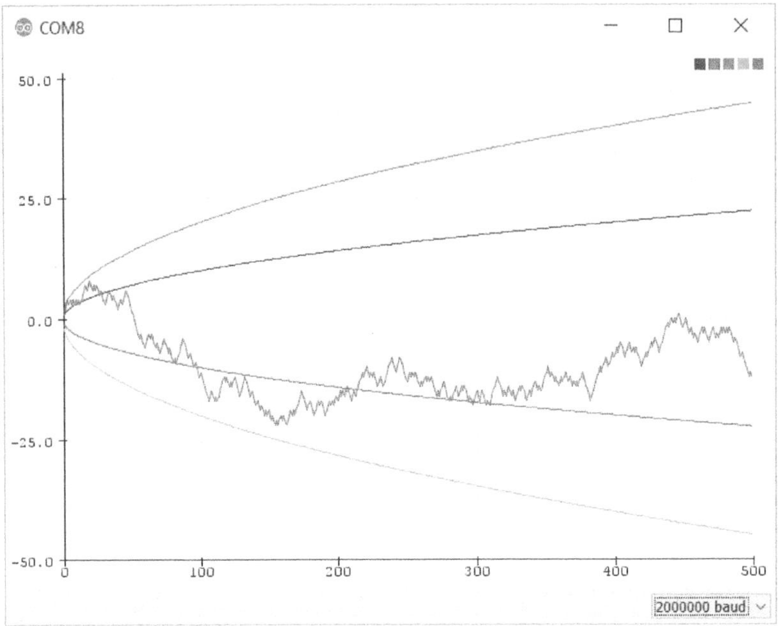

Figure 10.1. An example of my precognitive test. I guessed wrong more often than correctly. But, is there something to my score, or is it equivalent to chance?

I used a delay of 200 msec. This was short enough to speed the tests along but long enough that I can click the switch just once and run just one trial.

Also, I added a delay of 30 seconds at the end of the run before the beginning of the next run. This is plenty of time to review the results.

If you want to start the next run before the 30 seconds are up, just close the serial plotter and open a new one. Opening up a new plotter window will restart the sketch.

If, at the end of the run, you want to record the random walk result of your test, all you have to do is a screen capture and save the result as an image.

10.5 Controlling the next coin flip: testing your *telekinesis*

To test your ability to control the outcome of the random selection of the blue or red LED, all you have to do is change the order of the operations.

Instead of selecting the LED color and *then* predicting the selection by clicking the switch, we will think the random color we want to appear and *then* press the switch corresponding to the color we were trying to make come up. Only after we have made our selection will the random number be generated.

We still compare the running sum of how many times we had the same color come up we were trying to make come up.

Try this experiment: Re-write the code from the last experiment to implement a test for ***telekinesis***.

10.6 Sketch: Can you affect the next coin flip?

After you have given it a try, take a look at my sketch.

```
int iRnd;
int iSum;
int pinBlue = 13;
int pinRed = 12;
int pinSwBlue = 2;
int pinSwRed = 3;
int iDelay_msec = 200;
int iGuess;

void setup() {
```

```
  Serial.begin(2000000);
  pinMode(pinBlue, OUTPUT);
  pinMode(pinRed, OUTPUT);
  pinMode(pinSwBlue, INPUT);
  pinMode(pinSwRed, INPUT);
  randomSeed(micros()+analogRead(A5));
}

void loop() {
  for (int i = 1; i <= 500; i++) {
    while ((digitalRead(pinSwBlue) == 1) and (digitalRead(pinSwRed) == 1)) {
    }
    if (digitalRead(pinSwBlue) == 0) {
      iGuess = 1;
    }

    if (digitalRead(pinSwRed) == 0) {
      iGuess = -1;
    }
    iRnd = 2 * random(0, 2) - 1;
    if (iRnd == 1) {
      digitalWrite(pinBlue, HIGH);
      delay(iDelay_msec);
      digitalWrite(pinBlue, LOW);
      delay(iDelay_msec);
    }
    if (iRnd == -1) {
      digitalWrite(pinRed, HIGH);
      delay(iDelay_msec);
      digitalWrite(pinRed, LOW);
      delay(iDelay_msec);
    }
    if (iGuess == iRnd) {
      iSum = iSum + 1;
    }

    if (iGuess != iRnd) {
      iSum = iSum - 1;
    }
    Serial.print(sqrt(i)); Serial.print(", ");
    Serial.print(-1 * sqrt(i)); Serial.print(", ");
    Serial.print(2 * sqrt(i)); Serial.print(", ");
    Serial.print(-2 * sqrt(i)); Serial.print(", ");
    Serial.println(iSum);
  }
  delay(30000);
}
```

All we had to do was literally move one line of code, where we created the iRnd value:

iRnd = 2 * random(0, 2) - 1;

to occur after the switch is pressed.

When I ran this experiment, my score is shown in Figure 10.2.

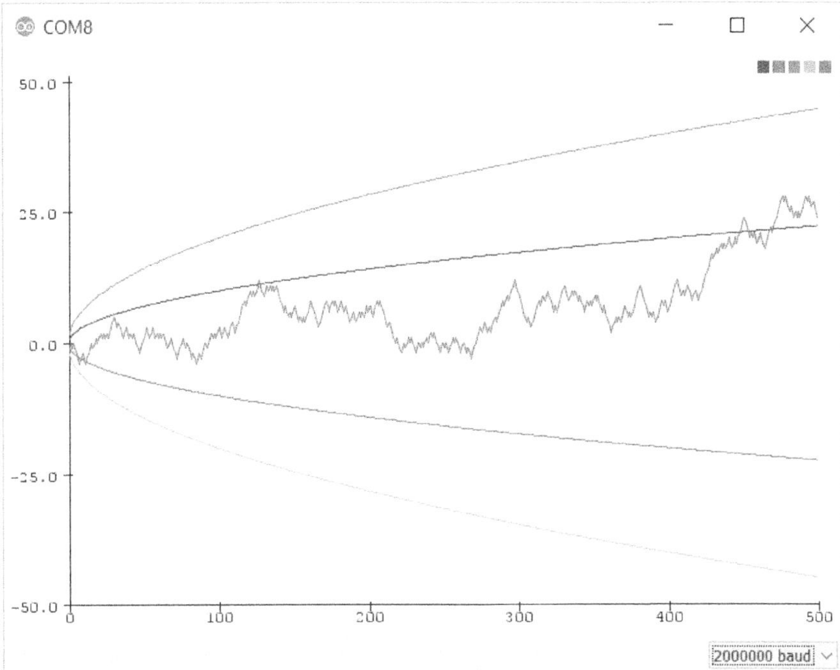

Figure 10.2. The results from my telekinesis experiment. I was not able to influence the LED color much above what is expect based on chance.

10.7 Analysis

When you do these sorts of tests, it's easy to fool yourself into thinking maybe you do have some precognitive or ***telekinetic*** ability.

There is a hidden assumption that if we do have such an ability, then the correct result should come up some percentage of the time.

In other words, our ability to predict or control the correct reading should happen some fraction of the time, like 5% or 10%.

This means as the number of trials grows, the number of correct occurrences will grow as well, proportional to the number of trials, n.

As we saw in our randomness experiments, the natural random walk deviation from zero also increases with the number of trials, but increased with $\sqrt{n}$.

If there is a real effect that increases as a percentage of n, this will increase faster than the square root, the value expected due to chance.

We can evaluate how many trials to perform to see a real effect come out of the random noise.

If there is a fraction of trials we can influence, f, then to get a value that is 3x the deviation expected from random chance, we would need:

$$n \times f > 3 \times \sqrt{n}$$

or, after a little algebra

$$n > \frac{9}{f^2}$$

If there is a real effect, however small, if you run enough trials, the correct guessing will always increase faster than the random values. To see the real effect above random chance, just run more trials.

For example, if you have an ability to make 10% more heads come up than tails, then you would need to run as many as n trials:

$$n > \frac{9}{f^2} = \frac{9}{\left(10^{-1}\right)^2} = \frac{9}{10^{-2}} = 900$$

How many trials should you run? If the effect is small, like 1%, so it is hard to notice, unless you perform a controlled test like these above, then the number of trials you need to run to show this result is above chance is about:

$$n > \frac{9}{f^2} = \frac{9}{\left(10^{-2}\right)^2} = \frac{9}{10^{-4}} = 90{,}000$$

If your ability to control the color that come sup is only at the 1% level, you would have to do 90,000 trials in order to see a real effect that is above chance.

We generally are running 500 trials. If we limit ourselves to just 500 trials, we are sensitive to biases, or abilities to influence more heads than tails with a fraction of:

$$f > \frac{3}{\sqrt{n}} = \frac{3}{\sqrt{500}} = 13\%$$

This means that if you have the ability to influence the roll of the die or the flip of the coin more than 14% of the time, you should clearly see the random walk exceeding the 2 x $\sqrt{n}$ in most runs. This is easily detected.

This random number generator (RNG) engine will test either precognition or telekinesis to the 13% level on a routine basis.

The more trials you perform, the farther from chance your results would fall. That's what doing science is all about.

Keep testing yourself, or others. This is how discoveries are made.

10.8 Summary of the commands introduced so far

Command	Description

`void setup (){`
 	
`}`
	This is a function that appears in EVERY sketch. Every command within the brackets will be executed just once

void loop (){
 	
}
	This is a function that appears in EVERY sketch. Every command within the brackets will execute over and over again.

`pinMode(13, OUTPUT);`	This command tells the Arduino that we are going to use a specific digital pin as an `OUTPUT`, as distinct from an `INPUT`. We use the pin number to identify the pin we want to setup.
`digitalWrite(13, HIGH);`	This command controls the output of a digital pin and makes it either a `HIGH` (logic 1, or 5 V) or a `LOW` (a logic 0 or a 0 V). Once executed, the pin value will be set to this value.
`delay(1000);`	This command for tell the Arduino to sit there, twiddling its thumbs, doing nothing for a duration of milliseconds as listed inside the (). In this example, the time interval to wait is 1000 msec = 1 sec.
// or /* */	Everything after these two forward slashes will be ignored by the Arduino sketch. We can use this add comments for our own benefit on any line. For multiple lines add them between the /* and the */ lines.
delayMicroseconds(1000);	Just like the delay() function, this function will force the Arduino to sit there and do nothing, for a time duration equal to the time, in microseconds inside the (). In this examples, 1000 microseconds = 1 msec = 0.001 sec.

`Serial.begin(9600);`	This command opens up the serial com link with a baud rated inside the (). In this example the baud rate is 9600 baud. The name `Serial` is an object, the serial link. The `.begin` is a verb, telling the object to get set up.
`Serial.print("Hello World");`	This command will print characters to the serial communications channel. Everything inside the () will be printed. To print a string, enclose the characters within quotes. After printing, the cursor will be left on the same line.
`Serial.println(" ");`	Does the same thing as the `Serial.print` command, but moves the cursor to the next line after printing the characters.
`int`	We use this to assign a variable name as a new variable. It is place at the beginning of the sketch. We have to assign a variable name to a type of variable. This command creates a variable that is a + or – whole number up to 2^{15} = 32, 767
`long`	This assigns a variable name to a + and – whole number up to 2^31 = 2,147, 483, 647. Use this when we expect to be counting very large number. You can never go wrong making all integer variables Long variable.
`float`	This assigns a variable as a floating-point number, which is any number having a decimal point. Use this command when the variable needs to have a decimal point.

`float Name[100]`	Declares an array using the [] to define the number of elements in the array size. Limited to about 301 elements in the Uno

`for (int i = 1; i <= 10; i++) {`
`  //execute this code if i<=10`
`}`
	This is a loop that causes all the code within the { and } brackets to execute for a certain number of times. Inside the () of the command are three sections, separated by ;. The first sets up the index that will step, and its initial value. The second, sets up the condition. While this is true the loop continues. When it is false, the loop breaks to after the }. The last section increments the index, i, by 1.

`sin(Phase_rad)`	This function returns the value of the sine of the number inside the (), assuming this number is an angle in radians. 2 x π radians = 360 deg.
`digitalRead(5)`	This command will read the digital value of the pin number inside the (), 5, in this example, and return the value as a 0 or 1 or false or true. Once executed, this command becomes the value it reads.
`millis()`	This function returns the value of the internal counter which is counting the number of milliseconds since the beginning of the sketch. Nothing is placed inside the (). This is a long integer. Every time it is called, it becomes the current value of milliseconds.

`micros()`	This function returns the value of the internal timer, which is counting up microseconds since the start of the sketch. The resolution is 4 microseconds. Nothing is placed inside the (). This is a long integer. Every time it is called, it becomes the current value of microseconds.
`while (i>1) {` `}`	This command will cause all the code within the {…} to execute over and over again, as long as the condition inside the (…) is true.
`random(min, max);`	This command returns a random integer value that is between the min value and the (max-1) value. The random number returned is a long integer.
`#include <SimpleDHT.h>`	The "include" command tells the Arduino to go to the list of libraries you have installed using the library manager and grab the one identified in the <…>. Then add all the commands listed in this library to the commands available for this sketch. It's like we are adding some new vocabulary words to what the Arduino understands.
`SimpleDHT11 dht11(pinDHT11);`	The command, `SimpleDHT11` is a specific command in the library we included in the previous statement. It tells the Arduino to create a new object, called dht11. The number in the () is the value of the digital pin that is connected to the DHT11 sensor. Once this object is created, we can make it do things by appending verbs to its end separated by a period.

analogRead(pinNumber);	This command will read the ADC channel in the (), as A0, A1, …A5, and return the value as an integer in units of ADUs. The resolution is 10-bit or 1023 different levels. It takes 112 usec to perform one analogRead(pinNumber); operation.
analogWrite(pinNumber, value);	Controls a PWM signal on selected digital pins which modulates the signal at 490 Hz or 980 Hz. The "value" is an integer from 0 to 255 that controls the duty cycle of the PWM signal.

if (this condition is true) {
execute this code;
}
	If conditional. If the statement in the () is correct, the code within the {} will be executed. If it is false, the code execution moves to the other side of the {}.

Chapter 11. The Next Steps

This second book in the ***Saturday Afternoon Low-Cost Electronics Projects Series*** focused on examples of using the features of the simple Arduino Uno to do real science experiments.

Best of all, every experiment used either just the Arduino or the Arduino and the multi-function board. Together, the total cost to explore every experiment is less than $8, shipping included.

In addition to learning some science principles, we also introduced a variety of coding principles, and their best practices.

You will use these best practices for software and hardware techniques over and over again in future projects.

If you want to go the next step, and learn some more hands on science and engineering, levering low cost electronics, check out the other books in this ***Saturday Afternoon Low-Cost Electronics Projects*** series:

Book 1: Arduinos without Tears: the ultimate, simplest getting started guide for Arduinos with six experiments in science and coding using nothing more than a low-cost Arduino.

Book 2: Science Experiments with Arduinos Using a Multifunction Board, exploring more than a dozen experiments using the Arduino and a simple add on multi-function board costing about $3. No wiring needed, just plug and play.

Book 3: More Science Experiments with Arduinos Using an LED Accessory Kit: exploring another dozen experiments in science and electronics using the Arduino and a simple kit of parts costing less than $3.

Book 4: Science Experiments with the SparkFun RedBoard Turbo, exploring more than a dozen experiments using the Sparkfun RedBoard Turbo, a high-performance data acquisition Arduino.

Book 5: Three Must Have Instruments for Every Lab: the missing manuals for the Arduino as a voltage source and datalogger, the Digital Multi-Meter (DMM), and the scope/function generator.

Book 6: Electronics You Should Have Learned in High School. Starting with the basics and establishing a firm foundation in current, voltage, resistance and power, simple circuits, voltage sources, I-V curves, diodes, schematics, measuring voltage, current, resistance, voltage dividers, capacitors and inductors.

You can find more details about these and other resources on my author's page on Amazon.com and my author's website, and my Hacking Physics Journal web page.

Better yet, subscribe to the Hacking Physics Journal newsletter.

Drop me a note sometime and let me know what you think!

About Eric Bogatin

Eric Bogatin is currently a Signal Integrity Evangelist with Teledyne LeCroy and the Dean of the Teledyne LeCroy Signal Integrity Academy, at www.beTheSignal.com . Additionally, he is an Adjunct Professor at the University of Colorado - Boulder in the ECEE dept, and technical editor of the Signal Integrity Journal.

Eric received his BS in physics from MIT in 1976 and MS and PhD in physics from the University of Arizona in Tucson in 1980. He has held senior engineering and management positions at Bell Labs, Raychem, Sun Microsystems, Ansoft and Interconnect Devices. He has written six technical books in the field and presented classes and lectures on signal integrity world-wide.

For more than 50 years, he has followed his passions of teaching and hands-on electronics by writing, lecturing and presenting workshops on low-cost electronics to makers, DIYers, hackers and engineer and scientist wantabees around the US.

For seven years, he has presented monthly Arduino workshops at Tinkermill, our local hacker space in Longmont, CO.

Eric is a prolific author, writing engineering textbooks, project experiment books for makers and science fiction novels. In his free time, he is also an amateur astronomer and a member of the Longmont Astronomical Society and the Boulder Astronomy and Space Society.

Contact him at www.EricBogatin.com or www.HackingPhysics.com.

Made in the USA
Monee, IL
06 October 2022

15364931R20132